Teaching Children
Who Are
Hard to Reach

Teaching Children Who Are Hard to Reach

Relationship-Driven Classroom Practice

Michael J. Marlowe
Torey Hayden

CORWIN
A SAGE Company

CORWIN
A SAGE Company

FOR INFORMATION:

Corwin
A SAGE Company
2455 Teller Road
Thousand Oaks, California 91320
www.corwin.com

SAGE Ltd.
1 Oliver's Yard
55 City Road
London, EC1Y 1SP
United Kingdom

SAGE Pvt. Ltd.
B 1/I 1 Mohan Cooperative Industrial Area
Mathura Road, New Delhi 110 044
India

SAGE Publications Asia-Pacific Pte. Ltd.
3 Church Street
#10-04 Samsung Hub
Singapore 049483

Acquisitions Editor: Jessica Allan
Associate Editor: Julie Nemer
Editorial Assistant: Lisa Whitney
Permissions Editor: Jason Kelley
Project Editor: Veronica Stapleton
Copy Editor: Brenda White
Typesetter: Hurix Systems Pvt. Ltd
Proofreader: Wendy Jo Dymond
Indexer: Sheila Bodell
Cover Designer: Candice Harman

Printed in the United States of America.

Library of Congress Cataloging-in-Publication Data

Marlowe, Michael J., 1947–

Teaching children who are hard to reach : relationship-driven classroom practice / Michael J. Marlowe and Torey Hayden.

p. cm.

Includes bibliographical references and index.

ISBN 978-1-4522-4444-0 (pbk.)

1. Problem children—Education. 2. Problem children—Behavior modification. 3. Classroom management. 4. Teacher-student relationships. 5. Effective teaching. I. Hayden, Torey L. II. Title.

LC4801.M36 2013
371.93—dc23

2012021033

This book is printed on acid-free paper.

12 13 14 15 16 10 9 8 7 6 5 4 3 2 1

Contents

Preface by Mike Marlowe

This is a text for future and current teachers of children who are resistant or hard to reach. Its focus is the philosophy, classroom practice, and teacher stories of Torey Hayden, a teacher of children with emotional and behavioral disorders, coauthor of this book, and author of eight books chronicling her day-to-day work in special education and child psychology. Hayden's first book was *One Child* (1980), the story of Sheila, a silent troubled girl, who had tied a 3-year-old boy to a tree and critically burned him. *One Child* was followed by *Somebody Else's Kids* (1982), *Murphy's Boy* (1983), *Just Another Kid* (1986), *Ghost Girl* (1992), *The Tiger's Child* (1995), the sequel to *One Child, Beautiful Child* (2002), and *Twilight Children* (2006).

All of Hayden's books are particularly helpful for understanding relationships. Her stories stress the interpersonal dynamics and emotional connections involved in working with resistant children and emphasize relationship skills, intuition, and the social milieu in changing children's behavior. Both new and long-term teachers need the perspective Hayden provides in her stories of classroom life.

This book reflects the growing interest in teacher education in building theories from successful practice rather than just trying to put theory into practice. There is increased recognition of the authority that derives from expert teachers' careful examination of real-life classroom events and the complexities of what it means to teach children. And there are signs of a renewed respect for the importance of *practice expertise* in building a knowledge base of teaching (Cook, 2012). Without turning to the work of reflective practitioners and their grounded knowledge, our understandings of what it means to teach children remain disconnected from the real world.

I first became aware of Torey, as her students call her in her stories, in 1992 when examining books for possible adoption as texts in a university course on the education of emotionally disturbed children. The last page of a paperback had an advertisement for Torey's books with the hyperbolic tag line "The World Needs More Like Torey Hayden." Beneath the ad was a coupon for ordering the books of this proclaimed "miracle worker." Curious, I put it in the mail.

What drew me to her work was the difference in her approach, as backdrop to her stories, to emotionally disturbed children in contrast to the primary approaches today. Current American research shows that classrooms for emotional and behavioral disorders in the public schools today rely on heavy use of behavior modification programs, which seem primarily aimed at achieving obedience. These classrooms have been described as curriculums of control, and they are widely viewed as ineffective. Here was a viable alternative, an approach that centered on relationships and appropriate social interaction and caring in a very real way.

I was also drawn to Torey's work by how her writing accurately portrays what it *feels* like to work with children, transporting me back to when I taught in classrooms for emotional and behavioral disorders in the public schools of Indiana and Kentucky. Here was a kindred spirit, as she articulated the feelings I had experienced—compassion and anger, joy and sadness, and enthusiasm and frustration. Her stories evoked thoughts, feelings, purposes, images, and aspirations not contained in the research bound texts I normally assigned in teacher education, so taking a new direction, I adopted three of her books.

This proved to be a popular decision with the students. They sensed the excitement of a writer who was there before they were and writes it like it really is. End-of-course student evaluations of the books were superb (e.g., "A wonderful learning source"; "I'm now a member of the Torey Hayden fan club"; "When in doubt I ask myself, what would Torey have done?"). Vicariously, students saw themselves in Torey's classroom stories; they imagined new possibilities for their own teaching.

Two decades later, I continue to use Torey's stories in teacher education and in doing so have distilled from them an approach to educating children with emotional and behavioral disorders, which could be termed the *relationship-driven classroom*. The crucial foundations of a relationship-driven classroom are the individual relationships between the teacher and the child and those among the children and the group or unit relationship. What sets the relationship-driven methodology apart from other methodologies is its active use of interpersonal relationships as a means of change.

The importance of relationship became apparent to Torey when she was a college student and took on work as an aide in a preschool program for disadvantaged children (Hayden, 2002). Torey had been given responsibility for Mary, a 4-year-old, who did not speak, was afraid of men, and spent the whole time hiding underneath a piano. Torey's charge was to get the girl to come out. The director did not tell Torey how to do that or what to do.

Torey began her relationship with Mary by lying under the piano with her and carrying on a long, very one-sided monologue while she just watched. When Torey ran out of things to talk about, she started reading to her. It took months to achieve a relationship with Mary and get her to speak again, but it did happen, and the connection between its happening and the long hours Torey spent apparently doing nothing more than spending time with her was not lost on Torey.

A second experience soon followed reaffirming the importance of relationship (Hayden, 2005). As a graduate student in special education, Torey devised a small research project in learning disabilities. She divided children with identified learning disabilities and poor reading performance into three groups.

In the first group, children were paired with trained tutors who used the most up-to-date learning-modality-based methods to help them improve their reading; in the second group, children were paired with an untrained college student who simply read books, magazines, and comic books to them; and the third group was a control group who had no special interventions. The tutors/college students met their children twice a week for half an hour, and the project ran for 6 months.

At the end of six months, both treatment groups had made statistically significant improvements in reading. Both groups improved whether the children were being actively taught or whether they were simply listening to an adult read. Torey's conclusion from this was not that we don't need to actively teach children to read but that the significant influence was human interaction, rather than the method used. The results of the study spoke of how much it matters to us that someone else is willing to take the time to be with us, that our problems tend to improve simply by being with people who pay positive attention to us.

Source: The previous three paragraphs are based on material in *Twilight Children* by Torey Hayden. Copyright © 2005. Published by William Morrow, an imprint of HarperCollins. Reprinted courtesy of HarperCollins Publishers.

These insights into the power of relationships shaped Torey's approach to teaching children in classrooms for emotional and behavioral disorders. Her focus is on human interactive concerns rather than methodological concerns. There is no best method strategy. She thinks about the child, not the model. She reasons and reflects on a case-by-case basis. Her practice is derived directly from experience, using relationship as a process. She asks, "Who is this child? And what affirmations and experiences does she need to make her more humane and strong enough to survive?"

OBJECTIVES OF THE BOOK

The book's purpose is to describe the philosophical principles that underpin relationships as a means of change and present the teacher skills and concepts fundamental to creating and maintaining a relationship-driven classroom. Hopefully, teachers will not only gain insight into how to implement a relationship-driven classroom but also become more reflective about the meaning of teaching and learning with at-risk children and grow and change, both professionally and personally.

It is not just teachers of special education, however, that we seek to engage with this book. The majority of students identified as emotionally or behaviorally disordered spend at least a portion of the school day in regular classrooms, and such children form a substantial portion of the school population. Federal child-count data reported annually by states confirms that in 2003 to 2004, there were approximately one-half million students identified as having a serious emotional disturbance or about 1% of the school-age population (U.S. Department of Education, 2006). But many experts claim that emotionally disturbed children are grossly underidentified. They estimate between 3% and 5% would be more accurate. Mental health epidemiological studies suggest even higher rates (Kauffman & Landrum, 2009).

The behavioral, social, and emotional difficulties of the students in Torey's books are variations of the same persistent problems that many general education teachers experience with their most difficult students. The knowledge and practice of a relationship-driven methodology will be useful to general education teachers in their efforts to understand and teach students who are resistant or hard to reach.

Most teachers strive to make emotional connections with their students. However, making this a priority can be difficult since the passage of the No Child Left Behind Act of 2001 and the demand for higher state test scores and accountability. High stakes tests are not likely to go away, and a relationship-driven classroom promotes both emotional connections and learning. We know that students are more likely to attend school and excel when they feel like they belong. Feelings of connection lead to greater effort, greater persistence, and positive attitudes. Feelings of rejection have the opposite effects.

OUTLINE OF THE BOOK

Chapter 1, "The Relationship-Driven Classroom," describes the relationship-driven classroom model and how it differs from the three most common approaches to childhood behavioral problems: the behavioral model, the market or business model, and the medical model.

Chapter 2, "Relationships as a Means of Change: Goal Versus Process Orientation," describes how relationships are a process, not a goal, and how process orientation—the ability to focus and work in the present—is at the core of a relationship-driven model of treatment and management of emotional and behavioral disorders.

Chapter 3, "Teacher Skills Needed to Develop a Relationship-Driven Classroom," describes the social skills needed to create strong and healthy bonds necessary for effectively using relationships as a medium of behavioral change and the philosophical principles which underpin and inform all action taken in a relationship-driven classroom.

Chapter 4, "Discipline," describes laying the ground rules for a relationship-driven classroom, how to respond when misbehavior happens, and how in a relationship-driven classroom consequences are not the only appropriate responses to discipline and control.

Chapter 5, "Positive Classroom Climate," describes how one builds into a structured routine the opportunities for joy and enthusiasm, expression of feelings, stress reduction and relaxation skills, and communication.

Chapter 6, "Teaching Relationship Skills to Children," describes the importance of actively teaching relationship skills to troubled children, who often need direct and active help in developing these skills to a useful level.

Chapter 7, "Developing Teacher–Student Relationships," describes the importance of teacher–student relationships and teachers acting as functional adults while showing their warm and friendly side.

Chapter 8, "Successful Peer Relationships," describes how the teaching of the social skills children need to make and keep friends and to be a valued member of group are built directly into the curriculum.

Chapter 9, "Successful Group Dynamics," describes five strategies to strengthen the classroom group: concrete identification, deemphasizing comparisons, group responsibility, group problem solving, and group celebrations.

Chapter 10, "The Future," discusses the implications of a paradigm shift for teaching resistant children, away from control models, toward a relationship-driven orientation.

Preface by Torey Hayden

Mike Marlowe and I met in a serendipitous way. It was 1998, and the Internet was just finding its feet. A friend at work mentioned to me that the night before she had been playing around with Alta Vista, then the most sophisticated search engine, and had put in my name. Following the links, she came across a message board for a university she'd never heard of, but there were a lot of my fans there, discussing my books.

Curious, I went home and did what we all do at some time or another on the Internet—put my own name in to see what was there. I found the message board my friend had been talking about. It belonged to Appalachian State University in Boone, North Carolina and had been put up by a professor of reading in the Department of Reading Education and Special Education named Dr. Gary Moorman. He'd created the forum for his students to discuss course work, and in this instance, they were talking about books that had inspired them to become readers. Someone mentioned one of my books.

The eerie aspect of the Internet took over at that point, because, of course, while such web pages often feel like local, private corners of the universe, the truth is, one never knows who's happened across it. Readers of my books from Sweden, France, and Japan, as well as other parts of the United States, started joining in with questions and comments, and soon they had monopolized the message board. By the time I came across it, both the course topics and the university students for whom the message board was created had long since been squeezed out.

While it was good fun reading the lively discussions, I was embarrassed to be inadvertently responsible for swamping some university professor's efforts to go about his academic business. Seeing an e-mail link at the bottom of the page, I sent a few lines to Dr. Moorman and apologized for what had happened to his forum. He wrote back, bemused. He had, in fact, forgotten all about the web page. He'd set it up for a class the year before. The course was long since finished, the students departed, and he'd simply neglected to take it down. That it was now so active with my fans was as big a surprise to him as to me.

At the end of his e-mail, almost as a postscript, Dr. Moorman said, "We have someone here at the university who will be very interested to hear I've received an e-mail from you. He's a professor in special education, and he's written four research papers based on your books."

That was my introduction to Michael Marlowe, that e-mail response from his colleague to my apology for having accidentally filched his internet space. Since that unexpected start, Dr. Marlowe and I have had many discussions about educational methods, trends, and philosophies, both in the teaching of teachers at the university level and in the special education classroom itself. These discussions finally culminated in a two-day conference in March 2005 at Appalachian State University wherein I talked about how my real-life classrooms had been set up and shared video footage of my work and various examples of my students' work.

I am humbled that Michael Marlowe has given my books such a meaningful application in the field and pleased he has been able to show the efficacy of using these kinds of stories in teacher training. However, I wish to avoid imbuing my books in hindsight with a gravitas they do not have. They are not and never were academic or biographical records. They are narrative nonfiction, written for people who have had little experience of special education and with the sole intention of sharing what I found to be an extraordinary world.

Narrative nonfiction is a subjective story based on true events, unlike academic, biographical, and autobiographical work, which are literal and hopefully objective records of events. What this means in regards to my books is that while the stories are based on real experiences, they are told from my perspective. It also means that in the process of telling the stories, I alter names, dates, chronological order, and location. I also reconstruct dialogue and details, and, occasionally, I composite characters. As a consequence, this means I too become a composite character in the books.

There were several important reasons for choosing to write the accounts this way, as opposed to straight autobiography. Some are philosophical. I wanted to open up what was then, more than 35 years ago, a very hidden world. Friends and acquaintances had reacted with surprise and occasionally horror to my decision to work in special education, and I was often asked why I wanted to "waste my talents" on defective, rejected children who would never amount to much. My first books were written in response to this comment. I endeavored to open this world up and give wider access to some genuinely very beautiful people by writing in an accessible, narrative fashion. Later books were more issue oriented. Choosing incidents from my own experience, I attempted to exemplify the challenges and complexities surrounding certain topics in a way to which general audiences could relate. For example, I wrote *Ghost Girl* in the mid-1980s, when false memory syndrome, satanic cults, and such were at their height, because I wanted to illustrate just how hard it is for professionals to make an accurate assessment of a child's behavior and how easily cultural influences can skew our interpretation. I wrote *Beautiful Child* because I wanted to show just how easy it is even for caring and involved professionals to miss child abuse.

Another reason for choosing to write narrative nonfiction is that it makes the legal issues more straightforward to deal with. While it has been my practice to get signed consents and to give main characters the option to proof my manuscripts, the fact remains that some people do not want to be portrayed and refuse permission. There are also complex legal issues related to writing about minors. Narrative nonfiction allows people to be left out of the account entirely, when necessary, and the story reconstructed around them.

In other instances, people will give their consent to be portrayed but only if they are not in any way identifiable. As events in the stories occasionally render everyone directly involved easily identifiable, it is then necessary to composite characters in order to meet this legal requirement.

The other major reason for choosing to write narrative nonfiction instead of autobiographical nonfiction is the ethical consideration surrounding this kind of story. When one is hired as a teacher, there is an implicit expectation of confidentiality about what happens in the classroom. This is particularly important because the majority of those involved are children and not capable of giving informed consent. In this era of reality television and celebrity gossip, we're no longer clear about what constitutes privacy and what constitutes exploitation, but as someone in a position of trust, it is important to be very respectful of these boundaries.

In addition, while I present the classroom experiences as my perspective of what happened, and this thereby gives me some degree of ownership of these events, the fact remains that unlike stories in the *pain memoir* genre, I am not writing about my own abuse, emotional distress, or affliction. My stories are about other people's suffering. It is a very fine line between sharing worthwhile experiences for the greater good and exploiting others for personal gain, and I do not want to cross over it.

A further ethical consideration is the ongoing impact of the books. I worked with vulnerable children in public school situations. These children had no choice about being in my care nor about being taught by me. Several were still minors when I wrote the books that included them, so they were still incapable of signing informed consents for themselves and had no real choice about whether they appeared in my stories. Many of the events in the books are of a highly personal nature and often related to significant suffering. In real life people grow, change, and move on. We acquire new ways of coping; we outgrow childish behaviors; we gain insight; we learn how to move past painful experiences; and consequently, we progressively mature into different people. This doesn't happen to characters in books, however. They are permanently trapped in their 300-page worlds, their experiences as new and raw as when they happened. It is common—and normal—for a new reader to feel as if the events in the story have just taken place, because to him or her, they have. Readers typically react as if the people in my books are personally known to them because they themselves have been personally affected. So it is necessary to provide a protective space around the 6-year-old character in a book so that readers' enthusiasm does not unintentionally wound the 40-year-old person she's become.

The other important distinction between narrative nonfiction and academic nonfiction is that ultimately it makes me more a storyteller than an educator. I did not write any of the books to illustrate my prowess at teaching, to give a literal blueprint of my experiences, or to suggest that I have special techniques that others should follow. My formal career as an educator was only 12 years long, whereas my formal career as a writer has spanned more than 30 years. While I like to think that I was a good teacher during my time in the classroom, and I also like to think that my teaching career continues to this day in the larger classroom-without-walls of my readership, there are many, many teachers out there who are as talented or more talented at teaching than I am. I know. I've seen them at work. The real difference between them and me is that I can write. That is my true gift, that ability to bring an audience with me and let them experience what I experience. It is crucial readers of this book are able to discriminate between these two skills—teaching and writing—and thereby understand that at no time do I claim special mastery. My books are just stories of life in the classroom. There are millions of classrooms out there, millions of earnest, committed teachers working in them. The only thing that really distinguishes me is that I have a voice.

Dr. Marlowe has done a remarkable job of distilling a consistent methodology from my stories. He, however, is the true architect of this approach. I am both astonished and humbled that he could see what gave me heart so clearly and create from it a substantial, verifiable process. I am honored to be part of this process and hope that with it we can in some small way signpost a viable path through a complex and often disturbing world.

About the Authors

 **Michael J. Marlowe** is a professor of special education at Appalachian State University in the scenic Blue Ridge Mountains of western North Carolina. He has also taught special education at the University of Wyoming and Tennessee Technological University. He specializes in coursework in emotional and behavioral disorders and classroom management.

Prior to university teaching, Mike taught children in classrooms for emotional and behavioral problems in the public schools of Indiana and Kentucky.

Mike has published extensively and presented at national and international conferences on Torey Hayden's approach to teaching children with emotional and behavioral problems. Mike and his artist wife Susan have three children, who all live far away: Auckland, New Zealand; Los Angeles; and Denver. He enjoys nature, hiking with his yellow lab, Gracie, and an occasional round of golf. Questions or comments can be directed to marlowemj@appstate.edu.

Born in Montana, **Torey Hayden** has spent most of her adult life working with children in distress. Starting out as a special education teacher for children with emotional difficulties, she latterly moved into research and therapeutic intervention, specializing in psychogenic language disorders. Now living in Great Britain, she provides counseling and advice services for several child-oriented charities.

Torey is the author of several internationally best-selling books about her experiences as a teacher and a therapist, such as *One Child, Ghost Girl,* and *Just Another Kid.* She also has written three novels and *The Very Worst Thing,* a story for 8- to 12-year-olds.

1

The Relationship-Driven Classroom

The most importance force in the relationship-driven classroom model, of course, is the relationship. The emphasis in the classroom is not on obedience but on appropriate social interaction. The goal is for appropriate social interaction to generate appropriate behavior. For this model to work, relationships become an important part of classroom structure. The relationship between the teacher and the child and the relationship between the children are the two most important components of this model. Proactive moves are made to ensure that the classroom, once filled with children, will engender appropriate relationships.

It usually takes about 8 weeks for relationships between the teacher and child and the relationships between the students to begin to gel. The interceding period is taken up with boundaries testing, getting acquainted, and fear reduction. It also takes that long for routine to become familiar and for separate individuals in the group to become a whole.

This makes sense!

1

To examine any approach it is worth considering the *how, who, what, where, and when* of it:

- How is the approach to maladaptive behavior conceptualized?
- Who is perceived as having responsibility for the problem?
- What has to happen in order for change to take place?
- Where does responsibility for change lie?
- When does the change take place?

Behavior = misconception

In the relationship-driven classroom model, inappropriate behavior is seen as a teaching opportunity. A very large amount of misbehavior occurs because the child simply does not know to behave differently, because he has misconceptions about how he should behave, or because he has misconceptions about himself. These situations are not corrective occasions. They are teaching opportunities. Functional behavior is taught actively via the teacher–child relationship and latterly peer to peer in order to give children experience of the appropriate behaviors they are to use.

In the relationship-driven classroom, problems are co-owned. It's not your fault, it's not my fault, and we are working on this together. Responsibility is shared or interconnected. The child and the teacher are on the same team against the inappropriate behavior. Throughout the entire paradigm of the relationship-driven model this is the goal. It's the teacher and the child on one team versus the behavior. It is never the teacher on one team against the child and his or her behavior.

For change to take place, the teacher must first form a relationship with the child. This is the only context in which change can take place. The cornerstone of this relational approach is commitment. It is the unequivocal commitment of one individual to another that evokes positive change. Children have to have this type of relationship if they are going to move forward. They need the esteem that comes only from knowing others care about them and that others value them sufficiently to commit to them. They need to know that while significant others may have been unable to provide this type of commitment, it does not mean they are unworthy of it.

In *One Child*, Torey changes Sheila's behavior by forming a relationship between them. Sheila changes because it matters to Torey that she change. This relationship gave her the energy to try to change that she didn't manage before because it now mattered to Torey. Although Sheila was able to internalize her changes eventually, in the beginning the change happened because of the interface between the two of them and because Torey made it apparent that it was important to her that Sheila change.

In the relationship-driven classroom, responsibility for change is shared. As a consequence, responsibility for change drifts away from individuals, away from individual ownership of problems, and away from individual change to the relationship interface and how the teacher and child relate. It is the child's and the teacher's responsibility to sort the problem out, and there are many things teachers can do to help ranging from teaching, role modeling, therapy, and supervision to just plain, good old caring. An amazing amount of change can be brought about by one single person caring enough about one single other.

Finally, in the relationship-driven classroom model, change is present oriented because relationships can only exist in the present. If the relationship is in the past, you can't change anything, can you? If the relationship is in the future you can't change anything. So change within a relationship-driven model is happening right now. This model uses a relationship-oriented vocabulary. It tends to use words like *sense, love, acceptance, tolerance, nonjudgmental, understanding, commitment,* and *helpful.*

Since relationships can only exist in the present, what you are working on *now* is what is being changed. Change is open-ended. You do not know the outcome. And no one can know the outcome. Consequently, you remain hopeful in this model because none of us knows what really can happen. None of us can see the future. And because of this present orientation there is considerable room for flexibility because you're always present. You are always monitoring what is happening, and you can change if it is necessary.

THE TEST FOR TRUTH

The new gold standard for evidence is that an idea from one field fits with ideas drawn from other realms of experience. This is called consilience by philosophers of science (Wilson, 1998, as cited in Brendtro, Mitchell, & McCall, 2009). Consilience links findings from separate fields to discover simpler universal principles. Consilience requires that truth be tested against the multiple perspectives of science, experience, and universal human values. When we tap varied perspectives, the big picture becomes clear.

A relationship-driven classroom model meets the test of consilience. It is supported by related knowledge from (1) natural science, (2) social science, (3) practice expertise, (4) the voices of youth and their families, and (5) universal values of respect and human dignity.

To start, biological science reveals that the brains of children have inbuilt attachment programs which strongly motivate them to seek out positive bonds with caring adults (Cozolino, 2006). The need for attachment permeates all of our relationships; it is designed into our DNA (Szalavitz & Perry, 2010).

Second, social science research in both teaching and therapy shows the power of relationships. Teachers with varied teaching styles can be successful if they develop positive relationships with their students (Morse, 2008; Pianata, 1999; Vitto, 2003). Likewise, a common element within all forms of effective psychotherapy and counseling is a respectful, valuing, and empathetic bond between therapist and client (Corey, 2000; Hubble, Duncan, & Miller, 1999). Psychiatrists and psychologists call such a relationship between the therapist and client the therapeutic alliance. A similar bond—a pedagogical alliance—between teacher and student is similarly powerful (Danforth & Smith, 2005).

Third, practice expertise from the successful experiences and the collective wisdom of youth care work pioneers demonstrates the power of relationships. The hallmark action research of Fritz Redl, David Wineman, Nicholas Hobbs, and William Morse, early leaders in the education of children with emotional disturbances, shows that real behavior change is facilitated by relationships (Brendtro, 2008). Nicholas Long (2008), coauthor of six editions of *Conflict in the Classroom* with Morse, states that "if we are not successful in developing interpersonal bonds with youth, then all subsequent treatment and pedagogical techniques are mechanical. It is like racing a car engine without any oil. It is not going very far before it heats up and shuts down" (p. 57).

Fourth, experience includes not only practice expertise but also the often ignored firsthand knowledge from youth and their families. Werner and Smith (1992) studied Hawaiian children with multiple risk factors (poverty, strained parental relationships, and poor role models) for 40 years. They found that one out of three of these children developed into competent adults. They then studied the children who were able to succeed despite living with much stress and adversity and identified factors that were present in these successful children; these factors form the basis of resilience. Werner and Smith found, among other things, that these children often credited a favorite teacher who went beyond academics and became a mentor, confidant, and positive role model for personal identification.

Likewise, a national survey of 12,118 adolescents by Resnick et al. (1997), in an article titled "Protecting Adolescents from Harm," found having an adult who was supportive to them was the strongest protective factor. The adult was someone the youth could count on for understanding, advice, and support. Teachers were among those adults mentioned most frequently as the source of this support. Families of troubled youngsters also consistently reported that what was significant about residential programs serving their children was that workers made them feel like they were important, like they cared (Garfat, 2010).

And finally, values of human dignity motivate us to create caring environments where all young persons are treated with respect and given the opportunity to fully develop their potential (Seita, Mitchell, & Tobin, 1996). Humans are innately disposed to treat others the way they want to be treated. This, of course, is the golden rule, which is universal across all major religions.

CONTROL-DRIVEN CLASSROOMS

Given the consilience of these views about the tremendous power of relationships, it is puzzling why relationships have not been a central focus in classrooms for emotional and behavioral disorders in recent decades. Since the 1970s, there has been a marked shift away from milieu models toward models which favor control. This preoccupation with control was first reported by Knitzer, Steinberg, and Fleish (1990) in their national investigation into programs for emotionally disturbed children; the self-contained classrooms they studied were dominated by *curriculums of control*. The curriculum emphasis was often on behavioral management first with a central concern on behavioral point and level systems. These behavior modification systems seemed largely designed to help maintain silence in the classroom, not to teach children how better to manage their anger, sadness, or impulses. Similar observations about this preoccupation with control have been made by numerous scholars who observed classrooms for emotional and behavioral disorders in North America (Brendtro & Brokenleg, 2007; Brendtro, Brokenleg, & Van Bockern, 2002; Cambone, 1994; Danforth & Smith, 2005; Morse, 2008; Nichols, 2007, VanderVen, 2009).

Most current American programs are based on two philosophical approaches, both of which emphasize control—the behavioral model and the market or business model.

BEHAVIORAL MODEL

This approach to dealing with behavioral problems comes from the scientific community. It takes its philosophical base from B. F. Skinner's research in the 1940s, 1950s, and '1960s wherein all behavior is conceptualized as resulting from external, discreet, observable *A-B-C chains* comprised of an antecedent to the behavior, the behavior itself, and the consequence of the behavior. The jargon is that of the laboratory: observation and data.

In the early years of this model, special education classrooms were regarded as types of laboratories, using strict scientific methods to discern antecedent behaviors and alter outcomes by strict manipulation of positive or negative consequences. Latterly, many classrooms established in using behavioral models have segued into the market model through use of token economies and now operate on a cross-breed version of these two models.

In this approach, responsibility for the problem is externalized. A child behaves the way he does because externally observable, discreet antecedents are causing externally observable, discreet behavior. Responsibility for change in this model is thus also external. Behavioral change is initiated, imposed, and controlled by others; and while the child may have the chance for input, responsibility is generally externalized to the point that the child's cooperation, permission, or even knowledge of the proceedings is not necessary. This external orientation of responsibility means that behaviorism is a *control* model (e.g., others control the factors responsible for bringing about acceptable behavior).

The behavioral model is *future oriented*. Change takes place when the inappropriate A-B-C chain is broken and a new, more appropriate one put in its place. Normally this is done by altering consequences. There is virtually no flexibility in this model when it comes up against exceptions or situations where it needs to adapt in the present. The strict adherence to discerning, then manipulating the A-B-C chain, and observing results means adaptation can only take place in the future, after the prescribed A-B-C chain has been completed and observed to fail.

MARKET OR BUSINESS MODEL

This approach to dealing with behavioral problems comes from the business world. The special education classroom is regarded as a management economy. Behaviors become a commodity. The jargon of this model is that of the business place: assessment, contracts, goals, and accountability.

In this approach, responsibility for the problem becomes an issue of *ownership*. Responsibility moves from an abstract concept to a concrete possession. Identifying the owner of the problem by default identifies the behavior as a discreet, observable entity, rather than leaving open the possibility that responsibility is shared or interconnected. Once ownership is determined, then trading begins. Behaviors are controlled and changed by being assessed and valued. Contracts are then drawn up with clear, concrete goals of change in exchange for something of equal value by another party.

Responsibility for change in this model is external. Behavioral change is normally initiated, imposed, and controlled by others, and there is little scope for the child to do more than agree to the conditions of the contracts, although the occasional good or creative bargainer can increase his pay off. This approach is thus also a control model, focusing on the use of external control to bring about acceptable behavior.

The market model also tends to be *future oriented*. Change takes place when goals or targets are reached, and these always exist in the future. So this approach focuses on what the child *will* be doing. Consequently, there is limited flexibility when this model comes up against exceptions or situations where it needs to adapt because the payoff is in the future and to vary from a contract is to break it.

MEDICAL MODEL

The other common approach to behavioral problems is, as the name implies, derived from the medical world. The special education classroom in this instance is regarded as a place of treatment. Behaviors become symptoms of illness. The jargon of this model is that of the medical world: disease, genetic disorder, intervention, and prescription.

Responsibility for the problem is a mirror opposite to the market model in that it is characterized by complete lack of ownership. Responsibility is depersonalized to the point where it becomes an act of God, nature, or genes.

Behaviors are controlled by prescribed drugs and therapies. Responsibility for change in this model is externalized. The child is a victim of something completely beyond her control. Consequently, this too is a control model, where acceptable behavior is achieved through the external control of medical intervention.

The medical model tends to be *past oriented*. This approach focuses on dealing with an irrevocable event or events, such as genetic makeup or organic dysfunction, which have already occurred. This model has limited flexibility when coming up against exceptions or situations where it needs to adapt, as it is largely restricted to prescribing a different drug. The time frame required for some drug withdrawal further restricts its flexibility.

Perceived as the embodiment of rational thought and the building block of intellectual and economic advancement in the post-Sputnik era, science has become a philosophical force in its own right. Scientific theory, reduced to its most basic, involves identifying a problem, forming a hypothesis, and then objectively testing it as a way of determining the nature of reality. The results are thus regarded as reality. All three of these models share this scientific philosophy and are valued for their scientific traits of being *clean*, objective, and accountable.

The problem arises when we try to apply scientific theory to people. As convenient as it would be if humans had no internal environment to contend with, this isn't a possibility, and unfortunately, there is no way to objectively observe what is going on inside a person's head. We can observe what goes in. We can observe what comes out. We cannot, however, observe what is happening in between. The only mind we have direct access to is our own, and even that is often heavily clouded by subjective perception. We have absolutely no access to other people's minds. This hidden area, this one place we cannot directly, scientifically observe, often then results in what we call *under-determination*. This means, in essence, that whatever objectively collected data we come up with about someone reflects less than the total amount of information there is about that person because we do not have full access to all aspects of the equation. Consequently, for whatever conclusion we draw about the cause of a particular behavior or how best to change it, there will always be other equally valid and possibly incompatible conclusions that could be drawn.

For example, we might have a child who has been placed in a behavioral management class due to serious problems with concentration and attention. If we are following the behavioral model, we will observe the child and count how many times he gets out of his seat to determine there is a legitimate problem. We will then identify the A-B-C chain. Antecedent behavior is when the teacher hands out worksheets. Behavior is when the child gets up out of his chair to sharpen a pencil, talks to kids next to him, goes to look at stuff on the bulletin board, and so on. Consequence is that he doesn't get his work done. An appropriate intervention under this model would be to alter the consequence. For instance, if he doesn't get his worksheet done, he doesn't go out to recess.

Now while this has all been scientifically done—child observed, hypothesis of the problem formed, and solution put into place—the hypothesis based on this clean, objective data underdetermines the problem. In reality, this child comes to school each morning on a doughnut and a Coke. His family eats almost exclusively junk food. He's never made the acquaintance of healthy, nutritious food, and as a consequence, his brain is so deprived of nutrients it isn't functioning properly. There is no way, however, for us, who are observing the child clinically in the classroom, to determine this is why the kid can't sit still. As a consequence, our intervention may have an effect, indeed, it may even be very effective in the short term, but it is simply controlling the problem. It's not changing it.

Now we have a second child in the same class who also suffering serious problems with concentration and attention. If we are following a business model, we observe and identify the problem to determine the problem. An appropriate intervention would then be to arrange a contract with the child. She will sit in her seat and do Worksheet A, and in return she will be "paid" one star. When she collects five stars, she can choose a small toy.

Again this follows good scientific practice aimed at producing clear-cut, accountable results. But again, in the process it underdetermines the problem. In reality, Child B has a mother at home dying of breast cancer and a father who has sunk into deep depression. She has been shuffled around among relatives, separated from her siblings, and is concerned that they might all be placed in foster care. Consequently, she can't concentrate for worry and upset at the disruption. All we see upon observing her, however, is a kid who can't sit still. The contract may be successful in controlling her tendency to get out of her seat but because it has underdetermined the problem, it will not bring about a lasting change in her behavior.

And now we have a third child in the same class who is also suffering serious problems with concentration and attention. If we are following a medical model, we observe and identify the problem. An appropriate intervention is to prescribe a suitable medication for controlling hyperactivity, such as Ritalin.

Yet again, this follows good scientific and medical procedure and is aimed at a clear-cut, accountable result, but yet again, it underdetermines the problem. In reality Child C is being seriously sexually abused by a neighbor. This has made him tense and anxious around his teacher for fear this adult also may hurt him. Moreover, he is very worried about leaving his pet cat alone during school hours, as his abuser has told him the cat will be killed if the abuse is disclosed. All we see on observing him in the classroom and in the doctor's office, however, is a kid who can't sit still. The drug may make him physically less inclined to move about, but the problem has been underdetermined, so the drug is simply controlling a symptom. It isn't changing the problem.

There are three primary shortcomings, which contribute to the failure of all these models in the classroom. The first is an *emphasis on control instead of on change*. All three models are designed for behavior management. The presenting, observable problem is treated as if it were the complete problem, and no effort is made to acknowledge, much less address the existence of other interdependent issues, which have created or maintained the behavior but which cannot be empirically observed. The child is simply taught not to do something. While this is a pleasingly clean approach to the messy reality of human emotional behavior, it isn't particularly effective at teaching the child how to prevent its happening again. Thus, by using these approaches, the emphasis in the special education classroom becomes obedience rather than personal growth.

The second difficulty is an *externalization of the behavioral problem.* In all three approaches the behavioral problem is seen as something separate and discreet to the individual. This externalization makes it more straightforward to *control* what is happening because, when it is external, other people and resources can be enlisted in the task. However, it also makes it more difficult to *change* the behavior because inherent in externalization is the concept that it is outside the control of the person doing it. This weakens a sense of personal responsibility for it. We are responsible for ourselves because only *we* are ourselves, but our responsibility over other things decreases the further away from us they move.

Another negative aspect of externalization is that it does not allow for linking a behavioral problem with its etiology. Without considering and understanding behavioral etiology, at least to some degree, it is difficult to teach a child how to predict her behavior before it happens and thus learn how to manage impulses, anger, fear, or sadness in order to prevent future problems.

The third difficulty is that *focus for a solution is either on the future or in the past* rather than on the present. Concentrating on what *will* happen if the child completes a contract or engages in inappropriate behavior or concentrating on what *has* happened, which needs the amelioration of drugs or treatment, takes control for change out of the child's hands simply because the child, like all the rest of us, only exists in the present. For change to be effective, it must take place *now* for the very simply reason that now is all we have to work with. Now is the only time the child can behave or not behave, so now is the place he needs to focus his attention in order to prevent misbehavior from occurring rather than on a future goal or a past event or malfunction.

So, perhaps it is time to look at alternatives. Most successful, experienced teachers use a degree of relationship-driven methodology which they will have developed intuitively as part of their teaching strategy. As such, we are unwilling to refer to this relationship-driven methodology as *ours*. Moreover, saying it is ours immediately produces an us-and-them quality that implies to accept this requires rejection of the other models and thus disallows access to their constructive aspects. On the contrary, we feel the three current models all have much to offer, are helpful to know well and understand, and are entirely appropriate in certain circumstances. Our only complaint with these methodologies is, as expressed by Abraham Maslow's famous comment, that "if the only tool you have is a hammer, then every problem becomes a nail." All three apply the same response to every situation. Because we are complex and individual creatures, this one-size-fits-all approach does not allow for the depth, breadth, and flexibility of response required if we want to *change* the behavior of a diverse group of people rather than simply control it.

2

Relationships as a Means of Change

Goal Versus Process Orientation

Before launching into discussions of the practical strategies of a relationship-driven classroom, it is worth taking time to discuss the general philosophy that underpins relationships as a means of change. When choosing how to frame our lives, how to find motivation to strive for betterment, and how to gain fulfillment and meaning from what we do, we use one of two basic orientations: *goal orientation* or *process orientation*. Both orientations are a normal part of human behavior. Sometimes they are imposed externally by our environment. Sometimes we generate them internally. We all have experience of both. We all use both on a daily basis and, indeed on occasion, both orientations are present in the same activity.

Our experience, however, is that most people have a personal preference for one orientation over the other and will usually default to this orientation when starting something new or when organizing themselves during an ongoing activity. Similarly, societies in general also have a preference for one orientation over another, and this enculturation can strongly influence our facility to motivate and realize ourselves.

In *goal orientation,* behavior is motivated by the desire to achieve a goal. Motivation is generally extrinsic; that is, it is imposed on us from outside ourselves (either directly from our family, our community, or our culture or indirectly from what our family, community, or culture has taught us and we've internalized), and it derives from achieving the perceived positive consequences or avoiding the negative consequences of not achieving the goal. Fulfillment is usually concrete and occurs when the goal is reached.

The focus of goal orientation is always in the future, because a goal can only exist in the future. Once a goal is achieved, it has become part of the present. It is no longer a goal and thus no longer motivating because the consequences have occurred. For example, if your motivation to complete a puzzle is to receive a chocolate bar, that chocolate bar, as long as it is still in the future, remains motivating. However, once you are eating the chocolate bar—in other words, once the chocolate bar is in the present and not in the future—that particular chocolate bar is no longer a good source of motivation. You don't feel motivated to complete another puzzle once the chocolate bar is in your hand. Typically a goal does not continue to generate a sense of fulfillment in the present; so motivation to keep up the desired behavior drops off. Consequently, the normal course of action is to move back into the future again by setting a new goal (i.e., you get a new chocolate bar if you do the next puzzle).

GOAL ORIENTATION

Goal orientation is active. It is *doing mode* and employs cognitive, analytical, and intellectual thoughts as its methodology.

Many aspects of our lives are goal oriented. For most of us, our jobs are goal oriented, not only in the literal outcome of what we achieve or manufacture as a result of doing the job but also in our motivation for doing it. Most of us work to earn a reward for our efforts in the form of a pay check. This goal is reset each week or month to keep us motivated to do our job, and most of us would cease to do our work if the paycheck ceased. Education is also goal oriented for many people, particularly in youth. When young, we learn things in order to get good grades, as achieving this goal rewards us with praise, positive attention, and recognition from people who are important to us. Latterly, we learn in order to get a degree or accreditation. Achieving this goal rewards us with a better-paying job. For many people, once these goals have been achieved (e.g., in the present) they cease to be motivating, and formal education stops and is not undertaken again. Any time we do something for the outcome or the end product, that is goal orientation.

In *process orientation*, behavior is motivated by the meaning and fulfillment found within the experience or process itself rather than the outcome. Motivation is intrinsic. In other words, motivation comes from inside ourselves and happens because the experience itself is satisfying and meaningful. Consequences or outcome of the experience may reinforce the behavior, but they are not at the heart of this orientation. Fulfillment comes instead from awareness and appreciation of having the experience while it is happening.

The focus of process orientation is always present oriented, because, as we only exist in the present, it is only possible to participate in what is happening right now. We are physically incapable of experiencing something that is in the future or the past. We can remember it, imagine it, dream it, or wish for it, but we can't experience something in any time except now.

Using the puzzle example from a previous paragraph, if you are doing it as a process-oriented activity, you are not putting it together to see the completed picture or to see how quickly you can complete it, which is what would be happening if it were a goal-oriented activity. Instead, you put the puzzle together for the enjoyment of putting the puzzle together. The process itself is enjoyable, and this intrinsically motivates you to keep doing it.

PROCESS ORIENTATION

Process orientation is passive. It is a *being mode* and employs awareness and receptiveness as its methodology.

Many of aspects of our lives are process oriented. Virtually all of our social and relaxation activities fall in this category. We see our friends to *be* with our friends, to enjoy sharing the experience of being together. We usually go on vacation to experience new places or activities different from what we do at home. We listen to music or watch television to enjoy the experience of relaxation. All these things are process oriented, and the more fully we are present to them and not caught up in thoughts of the past or the future, which drag us away from our experiences, the more relaxing and fulfilling they are.

We can tell these things are not goal oriented because we do not engage in them to achieve something at the end it. We do not, for example, go for a nice night out with friends to get to the bill at the end of the evening. We do not take a vacation on a cruise ship to get to the destination. We don't watch our favorite TV program to get to the end of it. Any time we do something for the experience of doing it, that is process orientation.

One orientation is not better than another. It isn't possible to exist in a healthy and balanced way without both orientations guiding human behavior. Many undertakings contain both a natural goal component and a natural process component, and the two work in tandem. Rather like handedness, we suspect we each have a tendency for one orientation to be dominant over the other and, consequently, prefer this orientation to guide our lifestyle; but as with handedness, even though we naturally favor one hand, we would be deficient were we not to use the other hand as well.

Industrialized societies have always put an emphasis on goal orientation over process orientation simply because actively striving for achievement is the engine of progress. In recent decades, however, we have become increasingly weighted toward goal orientation to the point that in some sectors it has become the sole focus of daily life. Several things have contributed to this shift, but none more so than advances in technology because they have allowed us to more easily experience *instant gratification*, achieving our goal without having the *process* of waiting beforehand. In 1980, for example, if one took a photograph, one then had to go into a camera store or drug store to get it developed. Usually a week or more would elapse between taking the photographs in and having a chance to see the image taken. Today, with digital cameras and the Internet, one can not only see the pictures instantly, but one can also send them instantly right around the globe within minutes of taking them. No one has to wait. In 1980, if one wanted to communicate cheaply with a person in another country, one wrote a letter. Even if mailed immediately, it usually took a week or more to go abroad and a week or more for a return letter back, even if the recipient responded straightaway. Today one can e-mail, phone, or instant message friends, family, and colleagues in other countries, communicating back and forth with conversational ease. In 1980, if one wanted to see a film, the only choice was to go to the movie theater or wait until one of the three networks showed it on television. Now one can rent or buy films whenever one chooses, check one of the countless channels on TV, or download it from the Internet.

Time and distance seldom constrain us any longer from having what we want. Money still does, but technology has allowed us to do away with much of the process (the waiting stage) and go straight to the goal. Instant gratification is seen as advancement in technology and has become common reality in many aspects of our daily lives.

Another contributor to the shift toward goal orientation over process has been the crossover and spread of marketing theory into areas such as medicine, social services, and education. Moving away from older theories of human behavior that relied on intuition and interpretation, such as those of Freud, Jung, and Rogers, and entailed a long, slow process of talk therapy, we now prefer science-based theories, such as Skinner's, which reject the internal human landscape as integral to change and place the focus on what is external and objectively observable. This external, detached approach makes it easier to quantify people in the way one does products, and the services provided to people become production-line activities aimed at efficiency and precision in delivery. In turn this has given rise to such concepts as accountability-based performance, measured learning, league tables, classroom contracts, and time-limited therapy, all of which are solely goal oriented.

Again, it's important to point out this is not a polemic against goal orientation or the use of behavioral, marketing, or medical approaches to dealing with behavior problems and behavior management. All have their rightful place. It is instead simply an effort to point out that in the current culture, process has been repeatedly depreferenced in favor of goals to a point where very little time is spent in process.

So does that matter? If we can achieve our goals more quickly, is there anything wrong with shortening or cutting out the process when we can? How important is process?

Perhaps we can illustrate this best with a story. Like many authors, Torey has a website to promote her work. For a long time, it included a message board where fans could chat with each other. With members from over 65 different countries, the message board developed into a little community of its own, a little international microcosm. On one occasion a Norwegian lady asked for an authentic recipe for that quintessential American treat, chocolate chip cookies, as she was curious what *real* ones tasted like. Two or three American members duly obliged, and a small discussion ensued as the Europeans on the board tried to work out where to source ingredients uncommon in their countries and what the American *cup* measurements would be in metric. It was at this point that the Norwegian lady remarked how anxious she was to get on with trying this recipe because they sounded so delicious. One of the Americans then remarked, "Yes, they are really good, but it's been years since I made any. These days I always end up picking up the ready-made dough in the refrigerated section of my supermarket. I can't be bothered to take the time to make them from scratch."

Something about that small statement struck Torey. It takes maybe 20 minutes to mix up the dough from scratch and bring it to the same stage as the ready-made dough from the supermarket. And what? It might take another 10 minutes to put away the ingredients, load the bowl and beater in the dishwasher, and wipe down the counter afterward? This isn't a big investment of time. Most of us kill that amount of time in unnecessary or unfulfilling activities two or three times each day without thinking about it. Certainly it is much less than we averagely spend in front of the television each night. So it can't be literal lack of time. What was actually being said here? What Torey heard is "I want the outcome. I want the goal of cookie-making—the cookies—with as little input on my part as possible." In other words, I want the cookies *now*.

What is missing? What *is* baking cookies all about? What is in all that getting the bowl out, measuring the flour, beating the eggs, chopping up the chocolate, mixing it in the batter that one cuts out by buying the dough in the chill cabinet at the supermarket? It's the process. To create instant gratification, having the cookie *now*, one cuts out the process and goes directly to the goal.

Two things need to be considered here. First is the impact of the process. Current research into happiness, into that state of abiding contentment that allows people to respond joyfully and resiliently to life, indicates repeatedly that the happiness we attain from experiences, such as being with friends or going on a vacation, has a higher and much longer lasting impact on our well-being than does the happiness from attaining a thing, such as a new car or a TV. Now let's go back to our chocolate chip cookies. Think back a minute to your own childhood experiences. Almost all of us remember being in the kitchen at some point when our mother or another significant adult was baking, and many of us will have experienced being included, perhaps baking cookies with a grandparent, or perhaps making a birthday cake or some other special occasion food with a family member or friend. And what do we actually remember about this? For most people, it is the *experience* that is recalled—the *process*—the *making* of the food. Very few people remember actually eating it. If they do, even this tends to be remembered within the context of the process (i.e., being curious to taste it *because* they helped make it, being proud to present it to someone special *because* they helped make it), rather than in context of the goal (i.e., to eat cookies or to have a completed birthday cake).

The second thing to consider is the importance of process. What happens when we cut it out? In going straight for the cookies, what are we losing? How important *is* process to how we think, feel, and grow?

In our experience, the following skills can be identified as *process skills*, proficiencies, which arise during the process period, are maintained as part of the process, and are no longer active once we've reached our goal.

Organizational Skills

Think again of our cookies. In order to bake cookies, one needs to find the recipe, read the recipe, gather the ingredients, and perform the steps in order. The adult is usually directing this process: "Do this first." "Don't do that." Each time the child bakes the cookies again, these same aspects are reinforced, and each time he or she has a better idea of how to start, what is involved, and how to put those things together to get the desired outcome. However, if the child is simply given a cookie, thus short-circuiting the process, this organizational learning doesn't take place.

Sustained Concentration

The child is only going to have a nice, tasty chocolate chip cookie if he or she sticks with the process all the way from getting the bowl out to taking it out of the oven and letting it cool. A young child of two or three will have a hard time sustaining concentration through this whole process, but if one watches a parent baking with his or her child, you will hear the parent quite naturally teaching the child this skill by refocusing the child's attention on the task. "What do we do next?" "Do you want to put this in?" "What does this taste like?" Throughout the process, the parent encourages concentration to the task. And without this sustained concentration, the goal will not be achieved. A child of two or three will have trouble, but by five or six, most children accustomed to baking will happily sustain concentration throughout a baking session. However, no concentration skills are needed—or taught—when one leaves out the process and simply hands a cookie to a child.

Patience or the Ability to Wait

This is closely allied to sustained concentration. Patience is very definitely a learned skill. Things in life do not happen any faster than they happen. A freshly baked homemade cookie cannot happen without going through the whole process of making it. No matter how much a child may want it right now, she is forced to be patient. Again, it is hard for a 2-year-old anticipating a cookie to be patient, but if she has no choice but to wait, she will wait. This is the secret to patience. Repeated experience of having waiting as being a natural part of the process, of having no choice in reaching the goal any faster, teaches us how to wait. Patience is enforced on us. We might not like the experience, but we learn to do it because there is no alternative to the process. And as with all skills, we get better at it with practice.

Anticipation

Most of us are familiar with the old adage happiness is a journey, not a destination. In other words, happiness occurs in the process of achieving a goal. Anticipation plays a key role in the amount of pleasure we feel when the goal is attained (or dread, if it's an outcome we wished we could avoid!) to the point that often the bulk of the actual experience lies in the anticipation. It becomes a skill insofar as it is during this process of anticipation that we tend to engage in our most honest self-assessment and self-realignments to discern if we are on track for the goal. This anticipation of the outcome before it is achieved allows us to learn how to monitor our own behavior accurately and adjust it when necessary.

Persistence

Within the process of learning to wait is the kernel of another important skill—learning to be persistent—because persistence is nothing more than the ability to stay with the process an extra long time for the outcome you want.

Selective Attention

This is the ability to focus on one thing while ignoring competing stimuli. For one to achieve the goal of a chocolate chip cookie, one must attend to the task of finding the ingredients, mixing them together, putting them in the oven, and timing how long they are in there. This is not the time to play with the cat or answer the e-mail. If one does, there will be no cookies. Thus, one learns to selectively ignore the cat walking through the kitchen and the computer at the desk in order to keep to the process of making cookies. If a child is working with an adult on this project and becomes distracted, the adult will gently reorient the child, helping him keep his mind on the task at hand. Again, a 2- or 3-year-old child will get distracted quite easily from making cookies, but by 5 or 6, a child experienced in this process will be able to reorient themselves and selectively ignore outside distractions to complete the cookie making with little trouble.

Peacefulness and Emotional Calming

Being able to maintain one's focus on the process, to be able to be with what is happening in the present moment, has an innately relaxing quality. This quality is exploited to its fullest in such things as formal meditation and Herbert Benson's *The Relaxation Response* (2000), but it is inherent in all process-oriented activities. For this reason, virtually all of our relaxation activities are naturally process oriented and not goal oriented. Listening to music, going for a walk, talking with a friend, seeing a movie, collecting stamps, playing sports, building models, having dinner at a nice restaurant, and watching TV are all examples of things people do in their leisure time *for the fun of it*. When we do these things to relax, we do them, by and large, because we enjoy being in the *experience* of them. We enjoy the *process*. If one talks to a friend because one has something important to communicate to him, then that is goal oriented, but if one is talking to him as a way of unwinding after a difficult day or enjoying time together, one just talks. It is the *process of talking* which is relaxing. One might go out to a nice restaurant because one is hungry and needs to eat and that is goal oriented, but most of us go to a nice restaurant as a way of relaxing and enjoying ourselves. It is the *going*, the *being* there, the atmosphere—the process—which is fulfilling. In the same way, some people play sports solely to win. This competitiveness is goal oriented and it isn't relaxing. It may be fun and it's good exercise, but there is innate tension in striving to win. Most of us, however, engage in a sport, whether golfing, sailing, fishing, playing tennis, or other sports, because we find doing it relaxing and fun. Winning is a bonus rather than an objective. In playing a sport this way, we are enjoying the process.

Torey had a wonderful experience of the calming quality of process some years ago with a friend who had just given birth. She had experienced a very abusive childhood, so when she first had her son, she became extremely anxious that she would not be able to parent him properly. This was made worse by the fact the baby was colicky in the first 3 months and cried incessantly.

Torey came to stay with this friend for a while in an effort to help out. Hearing the baby crying in the wee morning hours, she got up to find her friend had the baby held against her chest in one of those Snugli child slings while she sat on the floor of the living room. She had a large, rather sophisticated coloring book of stained glass windows and a box of marking pens spilled out on the coffee table and was very carefully coloring in the windows. She explained that she had always found coloring soothing because it "gave you space not to have to think about anything." All the focus was on filling in the spaces.

What child colors today? Coloring books fell out of fashion in the late 1960s and 1970s because they weren't considered creative. And no, they're not. But when done as an activity of choice, they are calming.

Meditation works on the same principle. All meditation involves is learning how to be aware of what is happening right now in the present, such as the inhalation and exhalation of breath, without getting distracted by thoughts and following them, as thoughts inevitably lead us away from the present moment and into the future or the past. Meditation is nothing more than practice at staying fully in the process.

These are all important skills that children learn during the process period of an activity rather than the goal achievement period. When we focus exclusively on the outcome, when we strive for increasingly instant gratification and thus reduce or eliminate the process period in preference for the goal, we also reduce or eliminate the opportunity to acquire these skills, many of which play a crucial role in stable and balanced mental health.

Why is an understanding of the difference between process and goal orientation important to relationship-driven methodology? Relationships are, by their very nature, process oriented. We can remember or dream about a relationship, but we can only experience a relationship now, in the present moment. Thus, in order to use relationships as a way of changing behavior, we need to be oriented to the present process as opposed to toward a future goal. In other words, the relationship we have with the child *now* is used to change behavior as opposed to its being a reward or an outcome of the change. We are working with the environment, modifying what is happening *right now* by means of relationship skills, intuition, and social milieu, all of which exist only in the present. So it is crucial to be able to recognize the process as it is happening in the present moment, to be able to differentiate it from the future or the past, to be able to separate it out from external goals, and to be able to identify and use the fulfilling and rewarding aspects that take place in the process. Only then do we have the capacity to influence change.

3

Teacher Skills Needed to Develop a Relationship-Driven Classroom

Certain skills are fundamental to the success of using relationships in the classroom. They are much the same skills fundamental to successful relationships in general, and this list is by no means exhaustive. Rather, of all available social skills, the following are the ones we find crucial in order to create the strong and healthy bonds necessary for effectively using relationships as a medium of behavioral change.

SELF-AWARENESS

The key quality of self-awareness is the ability to step back from one's emotions and cognitive activity sufficiently to be able to discern what one is feeling and thinking. The other key quality is to have a reasonable understanding of why one does the things one does and how one's feelings and thoughts influence one's actions. Those skilled in self-awareness are able to maintain this awareness as they are thinking and feeling and are able to make use of that small space between antecedent action and their behavior. Consequently, they can actively choose how they will respond.

This crucial skill ensures that we can maintain our own behavior as a conscious action rather than a reaction to what the child is doing. It also allows us to monitor our behavior and make the almost continuous small adjustments necessary to discourage inappropriate behaviors and encourage appropriate ones.

It is the fundamental skill upon which all other skills and, ultimately, all personal change is based. Self-awareness always must be present. Without awareness of what we are doing, it is impossible to make any kind of significant or lasting change.

OBJECTIVITY

In goal-oriented methodologies objectivity is used in the scientific sense, referring to the practice of keeping assessment, intervention, and accountability solely in the external, observable realm in order to eliminate biased judgments. In a relationship-driven approach, *objectivity* is used in conjunction with its opposite *subjectivity* and refers to the ability to let go of the self-oriented point of view and to see things from either the perspective of another person or from a general perspective external to ourselves.

Mike had a little boy with Asperger's syndrome, and individuals presenting with this condition are denoted by their inability to see things from a perspective other than their own. He disliked ketchup immensely. With Asperger's syndrome, again, it's highly common for individuals to have acute physical sensations. As a consequence, this boy became very upset when other people put ketchup on their food because he had no ability to understand what they were doing. He believed they were ruining their food by putting ketchup on it. He could not see that from their perspective it was alright to them. The ability to see from another point of view requires self-awareness so you actually know what you are feeling is subjective.

In cultivating objectivity, we recognize three things: (a) that our own perspective is limited; (b) that the other person also has limited perspective, which will be unique to them and different to ours, because they have had different life experiences and circumstances; and (c) that there is *always* a *bigger picture* that is both outside these individual subjective perspectives and inclusive of them.

When self-awareness and objectivity work in tandem, they allow us to see our own perspective *is* our own, to step back from it sufficiently to discern others have different points of view that will feel as internally valid to them as ours does to us, and to be able to step outside both to view the bigger picture.

Objectivity is not the same thing as empathy. Empathy is emotional congruence—feeling someone else's experiences or pain as if they were our own. While this is often an admirable trait, it is nonetheless a subjective, not objective, behavior. Empathy does not involve perceiving from another point of view but rather subsuming another's experience as if it happened to us and experiencing it subjectively within our own framework.

ACCEPTANCE

There is a duality present within the relationship-driven approach. On one level it is all about self-awareness and objectivity, which means recognizing that what we think, feel and experience affects our actions, but also that we each think, feel, and experience differently. On another level, however, it is about recognizing that we are all, in fact, alike. Our differences are superficial. At our core, we are *all* much more alike than different.

Acceptance is a complex concept because it requires, among other things, that we hold two apparently opposite truths in mind at the same time: that we are different, but yet we are the same. In other words, while we each have our own subjective realities and we need to be aware of this, we must also remember that we all share the same basic humanity, no matter how different we may appear from the outside. We all experience fear, joy, pleasure, anger, and discouragement. We all experience pain, fatigue, arousal, hunger, and illness.

An understanding of this commonality allows tolerance and acceptance to develop, because it enables us to let go of fear about the other person's differences. We're hardwired to be afraid of things we don't know or understand. The ability to perceive common traits allows us to understand that the other person, however different, bad, or repugnant, is at the heart really just like us, and so we don't need to fear them. It helps us realize that however bizarre, incomprehensible, or misguided their actions, they are acting in an effort to feel better or avoid pain, just like we do. This helps us accept the child is not a *beast* or *inhuman* or *unreachable* and that within him or her there will be feelings, sensations, perceptions and experiences like our own. And if we can connect with this common ground we have a chance of bringing about change.

FRIENDLINESS

It isn't necessary to be an extrovert to make relationships work as a methodology, but it is necessary to be sincerely interested in other people and to find a natural enjoyment in interacting with them. External methodologies, where focus is solely on the maladjusted behavior and controlling it, are not dependent on personality characteristics of the teacher. In order for relationships to work as a means of behavioral change, however, the teacher needs a certain level of natural friendliness in order to be at ease forming relationships.

In addition to these necessary skills, there are seven philosophical principles that underpin and inform all action taken in the classroom.

1. Relationships Are a Process, Not a Goal

As the previous chapter was devoted to clarifying the difference between goal and process orientation, there is no need to expand further on this. Suffice it to say, relationships are a process. Consequently, it is essential to be comfortable with and skilled at process orientation, the ability to focus and work in the present, because this is at the core of a relationship-driven model of treatment and management of emotional and behavioral disorders.

2. There Is a Difference Between the Person and the Person's Actions

Most of the time we regard our consciousness as *me, the person*, because this is the seat of our awareness and the means by which we process all the information provided to us by our five senses. Consciousness alone, however, isn't enough. All of us will have encountered individuals with brain injury or Alzheimer's who still have consciousness, but the part that made them who they are is no longer functioning.

Who we are, what actually constitutes us as a person, is remarkably complex to grasp. While we innately know we're located somewhere *here* within our body, it's actually impossible to find. Each aspect we look at falls into the category of *part of me* but is never *me*. We can keep deconstructing, but we simply end up with smaller parts. We never find that single, magical essence that is *me*.

Both religion and culture step in at this point to provide an explanation for this paradox, and this tends to influence our perspective. In everyday life, however, most of us simplify our identity down to our thoughts and actions. "I am what I think." "I am what I feel." "I am what I do." This is a practical and generally workable method for coping in the concrete world with what is at its heart a very abstract matter. Nonetheless, it is important to understand what is actually going on here—that we *are* substituting concrete shorthand for a complex abstraction—because it has a powerful influence on how effective we are in dealing with problems.

If we start to deconstruct identity, it quickly becomes obvious that everything falls into the category of *part of me*. My consciousness is part of me. My arm is part of me. My DNA is part of me. My medical record is part of me. My family background is part of me. My cultural history is part of me. And so forth. No single thing is *me*. The reason for this is so simple as to be obvious and yet feels so intuitively wrong as to be unbelievable: The fact is there is no concrete *me*. *Me* is, in fact, just a collective term for a group of connected parts, some of which, like consciousness, soul, or history, have no physical existence.

This is most easily understood if we compare it to collective terms we are more used to thinking of as collective terms. For example, *the United States* is a collective term for 50 separate and individual states. None of the states in the union is the United States all by itself. Each is *part* of the United States. The government of the United States isn't the United States. It too is part of the United States. The foreign policy of the United States is not the United States. The history of the United States is not the United States, and so forth and so on. These things are all *parts* of the United States. The United States doesn't exist as something on its own. Instead, it is a collective term for 50 individual states, a government, a constitution, and so on connected together by various histories. The United States is simply the abstract term by which we identify all these different things as belonging together. *Me* or *you* or *Mike Smith* works the very same way. While they feel very solid to us, they are actually abstract terms for a body, senses, consciousness, intelligence, and more that are connected together by various histories.

Understanding this distinction between an abstract collective term and the concrete parts that make it up is important because, as the collective term is simply a concept, we can hold it constant in our mind. In the normal course of things, I remain me all my life. Mike Smith remains Mike Smith all his life. The United States remains the United States. Because it is simply an abstract term, it need not change. In contrast, the component parts will be changing all the time. My hair may go gray. I may lose an arm in an accident. I may speak a new language or take up the beliefs of a different religion. I am still me, however. The collective term, because it is a mental abstraction, remains the same while the parts are constantly changing and constantly capable of change.

Understanding this distinction between the abstract constant and the ever-changing parts that make it up is the essence of understanding the difference between the person and the person's actions. This, in turn, is at the heart of developing a tolerant and nonjudgmental attitude toward ourselves and others regarding the following:

- *The capacity to change.* If a person's actions were as unchangeable as his identity, then there would be little scope for his learning new or more adaptive behaviors because "he'll always do that" or "he won't change." Understanding that a person *isn't* her actions, regardless of the number of times she has engaged in a certain action, allows us recognize she has the capacity for different actions.
- *The capacity to forgive or to move on.* Both forgiveness and letting go, whether of past hurts done to us or of past things we have done to others, would be impossible, were there no genuine capacity for change. Understanding a person isn't his actions and that what has happened in the past does not constitute how the person will always behave or *who the person is* allows us to forgive others and ourselves of past transgressions and to move forward in a more hopeful and positive manner.
- *The capacity to understand difficulty in changing behavior is not due to willfulness or lack of will.* If we assume our self is a single, concrete entity, this then leads to difficulty in understanding the very common scenario of knowing the right action in a given situation but failing to follow through with it. A familiar example of this for many of us is "I *want* to lose weight." I genuinely want this. I know and understand the reasons why I should

lose weight. I know and understand what the right actions are don't eat too much and take enough exercise. I sincerely try to do that. Nonetheless, too often I eat chocolate cake instead of spinach or I watch TV instead of going to the gym, even though I know these choices are counterproductive and even though I know no one else is cramming the chocolate cake down my throat. If I regard myself as a concrete, single *I*, then the only conclusions that can be drawn is that either I have willfully chosen to do wrong or I am weak willed. But what's actually going on here is much different. I'm not this concrete, single *I* that I feel like. That's just a word. I am, in fact, this collection of many parts, and I am ruled by committee. Sometimes my conscious mind full of newly learned healthy behaviors wins the committee vote, but sometimes my family history that has made me associate chocolate cake with good times and happiness wins. Sometimes my blood sugar wins. Sometimes my love of cooking wins. We've all had experience of these internal committee meetings where one part of us wants one thing and another part wants something different. And if adult life should have taught us anything, it is that it is extremely hard to get *anything* done by committee!

It's very important to understand this *committee* aspect when trying to make personal changes, whether it is oneself making the changes or whether one is supporting others making changes. While for practical, everyday purposes our minds solidify us into the concept of one person, we are, in fact, a collection of parts that can be all too democratic in the way they go about things.

3. No One Chooses to Be Unhappy

We all want to be happy. We *all* want this. No one wakes up in the morning and thinks, "Wow, I want to feel miserable," or "What a good day to be anxious and oversensitive." Everything we do, no matter how odd or misguided, is done because we think consciously or unconsciously that it will to lead to our feeling happier. Of course, many of these things don't produce this desired result, no matter how endlessly we try them, but this is because we do not have the awareness or understanding necessary to connect our actions to the consequences of our actions. It isn't because we purposely set out to do something that makes us unhappy.

This is simply another way of saying "Everyone is doing the best he or she can." People engaging in difficult or destructive behavior do so in the erroneous belief that this will relieve their unhappiness. They are not actively trying to be unhappy. Instead, they are actively trying to be happy but going about it in an unproductive way, because (for whatever reason) they are simply not able to do differently at this point in time. It is crucial to understand this. A misbehaving child isn't willfully choosing to be unhappy. She genuinely hasn't come up with a more effective way of being happy.

4. Misbehavior Is a Teaching Opportunity

If everyone wants happiness and no one wants unhappiness, yet there is misbehavior that results in unhappiness, then it is safe to assume the person does not know how to do differently. If he did, he would be doing it, because unhappiness sucks. If, on the other hand, someone *doesn't* know how to do differently, then the appropriate response from those who do is to teach her how.

This single point is perhaps the most crucial difference between a relationship-driven approach and the other current methodologies. Their focus is on control of inappropriate behavior. The focus here is on teaching to change inappropriate behavior.

In perceiving inappropriate behavior as a teaching opportunity, we recognize that it is being both unrealistic and unfair to expect a child to be her own teacher. In other words, if a child knew how to be happy, she would be doing things to make herself happy. That she is not doing these things indicates she is either unaware of the behaviors required or has not mastered these behaviors. If the child doesn't know something or cannot do it, it is unreasonable to expect her to be able to teach these things to herself. It is, therefore, necessary for us to teach what is required.

Here is a core problem with control methodologies. Imposing external control does not provide the child with more productive, alternative behaviors. Consequently, as soon as control is lifted, inappropriate behaviors often resume simply because they are familiar.

Most, if not all, children in programs for emotional and behavioral disorders will have considerable familiarity with dysfunctional adults and dysfunctional relationships. In contrast, they will have little experience of functional adults relating appropriately. It is thus both unrealistic and unreasonable to expect children to disengage from difficult cycles of behavior on their own without first gaining experience of the functional behaviors they need to emulate. In a relationship-driven methodology, functional behavior is taught actively via the teacher–child relationship and latterly peer to peer in order to give children experience of the appropriate behaviors they are expected to use.

Some aspects of appropriate behavior are taught by the teacher through active modeling. For example, the teacher will model the behavior of a functional adult, including such things as

- a functional adult behaves consistently and predictably;
- a functional adult has clear, fair boundaries;
- a functional adult is honest, fair, and moral;
- a functional adult has realistic expectations;
- a functional adult takes responsibility for his own actions;
- a functional adults knows how to deal safely and effectively with her own feelings;
- a functional adult thinks about others' welfare as well as his own;

- a functional adult will actively take care of children and not let them get hurt or be put into dangerous situations; and
- a functional adult will help children maximize their potential.

Other aspects are taught to the child directly, such as

- how a functional person manages his/her emotions,
- how a functional person relates appropriately to others, and
- how a functional person handles change, unexpected, or negative situations.

5. Everyone Can Change

This belief is *the* foundation upon which all the rest of the relationship-driven model is built. Everybody has the capacity to change.

This concept is at the very heart of all teaching, whatever the discipline. A teacher is there to bring about change in the student. None of us would choose an occupation that we knew at the onset to be an impossible task. *Everybody can change.*

This isn't Pollyanna thinking. Pollyanna says, "Everyone will change." This statement is just as black-and-white as "He'll never change." What we want to cultivate is the ability to stay positive about the *possibility* of change and the recognition that we are not omniscient. It's easy to fall into using black-and-white terms like *always* or *never* in regard to difficult behavior. But in doing so we are implying that the people and situations we are dealing with are fixed and discreet, and therefore entirely predictable, when they are, in fact, constantly changing and connected to and affected by an infinite number of other things of which we have no knowledge, insight, or control.

Because we may not be able to see how change will take place doesn't mean there is no chance for change. We need to promote personal change as doable and, in the process, distinguish in our own minds the difference between "I can't do any more to help this person" and "No one can help this person."

6. Personal Change Is Very Difficult

Permanently changing ingrained personal behavior is extremely hard to do because of a little thing called habit. We are hardwired to "do things as we've always done them." Active learning takes place in one part of the brain, but once a skill becomes a habit, it switches to another part of the brain entirely and becomes *automatic*. Automatic behavior is more efficient (notice the difference between people learning to do a task and those who already know how to do it), and the familiarity of knowing how to do it is emotionally comforting. Most crucially for our purposes, automatic behavior is just that—automatic—which means it happens even if we don't have to pay attention to it. We are all creatures of habit, a large portion of our daily activity being made up by automatic behaviors that have become so familiar to us that we are no longer aware of what we do to execute them. Think of reading, for example. Anyone reading this book will be automatically decoding the letters and taking in the meaning of the words. It is difficult, if not impossible, to look at the words on this page as if they had no meaning or as if they needed to be put together based solely on the letter sounds. Reading has become so automatic for us we can't easily become aware of what we are doing that allows us to read.

This disconnection between action and our awareness of action that happens in automatic behaviors is the roadblock to change. Habit makes change arduous. This is true for everyone. Anyone who has tried to lose weight, give up smoking, eat more healthily, go to the gym regularly, or make some other personal change that is *good* will know how difficult it is not only to embark on the initial change but also to keep it up over the longer term until it replaces the original habit and becomes the automatic behavior. There are many contributors to this difficulty. Genetic makeup, personal history, cultural history, and environmental circumstances all factor in, as well as motivation and consequences. Oftentimes, these factors all interact to a point where it is difficult to tease out just what exactly is standing in the way of change taking place.

The most important thing to recognize is that it *is* very hard. For *everyone.* As a consequence, it is normal for the individual who is trying to change to make many approximations before managing the right behavior. It is also normal to slip up or fail many times before eventually achieving the behavior. What recognizing that it is very hard translates into is understanding that these approximations, slips, and failures are an expected part of the process rather than the outcome. Consequently, when we endeavor to change a child's inappropriate behavior, it is normal for the child to try but fail, to backslide, to slip up, to miss, and sometimes even to totally fail and come off the program. This does not mean that change is not underway nor that the change is impossible. It simply means we haven't reached it yet.

A second important aspect to recognize is that very few people can carry out major personal change alone. There are inspirational stories of the Herculean few who have pulled themselves up by their bootstraps and triumphed over tremendous odds to become successful and healthy people. These are the exceptions. The vast, vast majority of us need help to change, sometimes a great deal of help, and often repeatedly, because habits are incredibly hard to break. Consequently, we fail at the first, second, third, or two thousandth time and have to keep trying.

If we keep in mind that people do not choose to be unhappy, we can then surmise that if they continue to do something that repeatedly makes them unhappy, it is because, for whatever reason, they are simply not able to do differently at this point in time. The appropriate response to this is patience. It means that they need more help or more time or both, not that they can't or won't or don't want to change. Sometimes it may turn out that we are not the person who can provide that time or help, and if this is so, this is all right. This is an honest assessment of the situation. It is crucial to be able to recognize the difference, however, between "I am not the right person to help" and "That person can't be helped."

In our experience, the following conditions must exist before personal change takes place:

- *Genuine awareness the problem exists.* Until we know we have a problem and understand precisely what the problem is, we can't change it.
- *Perceiving ourselves as having choices* and, therefore, the ability to affect our lives.
- *Accepting responsibility for the problem.* This means moving away from blaming someone else ("If he didn't always make me so mad, I wouldn't do that." "If my mother hadn't treated me that way growing up, I'd be more able to do this."), finding fault in the environment ("It's the heat causing it." "It's my allergy/disability/disorder causing it." "It's the current government/school/mother-in-law's policies causing it."), or assuming at the onset that nothing can be done about it ("It's simply my personality." "You can't fight city hall." "I didn't vote for this government," or "I've tried before and always failed.").
- *Accepting the behavior is out of control.* This means recognizing that we are not managing to keep this behavior within appropriate boundaries on our own and need help to change, whether it comes in the form of teaching, therapy, support from others, insight from books or courses, faith in God, and so on.
- *Showing compassion for oneself.* This means developing the awareness that we didn't get into this situation because we are evil or stupid or chose to, but because, for whatever reason, we simply didn't behave differently at that time. This looks at first glance as if it is not accepting responsibility for the problem, but there is significant difference. Accepting responsibility means accepting the problem belongs to us and we are in charge of sorting it out, as opposed to shifting the blame to things or people we can't control. Having compassion for oneself means accepting there is a difference between the person and his actions. Yes, we *are* responsible for our actions, and

yes, we have done wrong, but this does not condemn us as bad, shameful, or hopeless persons. We are each simply a person, like every other person. It is our actions that are wrong or misguided, and it is the actions that need to change.

Without this crucial component, self-esteem tends not to regenerate during the change process. Consequently, the individual does not achieve as much sense of personal satisfaction from the change, because she perceives herself simply as a bad person who is *acting* good and is thus a *fraud* when performing the changed behavior. Any changes that take place without improved self-esteem tend not to be internalized as a result. They are done only to satisfy external sources and therefore tend not to last once the external control is gone.

- *Identifying realistic increments of change.* It is normal for the increments of change to be small and the more entrenched the behavior, the smaller they usually have to be for success to be maintained. Because of this, it is necessary and, indeed, crucial to reward approximations of the desired behavior as one goes along. It is also important for both teacher and child to be aware from the onset that it *is* entirely normal to have to make such small steps and that the person making the change should be encouraged to be positive about any movement in the right direction, however minute the increments.

- *Persistence.* Because habit is very powerful, it is normal to fail many times in the effort to change it. It is important to instill the concept that while we may fail many times, we only *become* a failure at the point when we give up. Psychological research backs up persistence as the vital key to successful personal change, whether it is in terms of things like losing weight, stopping smoking, or changing unwanted behavior. Virtually everyone who has been successful at making one of these difficult changes has had at least 20 failed attempts before the successful one. So the key to this step is changing the child's thinking from "I can't do this" to "I'm still trying."

- *Adjusting self-image.* As personal change starts to take hold, it will begin to impact the environment around the child, which requires a self-image adjustment. Consequently, it is important to support this changing image as it emerges. This means actively moving away from labels that point out the individual's inappropriate behavior, such as "the one who doesn't keep quiet" or "the fidgety one" to more helpful descriptors. It also means responding to the changed person as he or she is in the present, as opposed to how he or she was, not in a gullible way but in a realistic way that allows the new behavior to settle in.

- *Hard is not impossible.* The bulk of this section has been all about how hard personal change is because our tendency is to underestimate its difficulty and then become discouraged by what we perceive as failure. However, it is equally important to understand that as hard as it is to make a genuine change in entrenched thoughts or actions, this is not the same as saying it is impossible. Hard, yes. Impossible, no.

7. The World Is Complex

Black-and-white thinking—the tendency to perceive things as all-or-nothing and thus able to be put into discernible, discreet and permanent categories—seems to be a hardwired trait for humans. We categorize and generalize by nature.

Black-and-white thinking is easy to grasp because it requires we deal only with literal perceptions. Such concreteness produces a sense of certainty, which in turn gives us a sense of control over what we are perceiving. Just as we know exactly where we are physically with concrete things we can touch and see, we know exactly where we are mentally when thinking in black-and-white. People are good or bad. Issues are right or wrong. There's none of that fuzzy grayness.

Unfortunately, this way of looking at the world, secure as it feels, gives us a false picture. It is two-dimensional thinking in what turns out to be a three-dimensional world. In reality very little is certain, nothing is separate and disconnected, and everything is in a state of constant change. Thus, responding to the world as if things were definite, discreet, and permanent results in frustration and failure because not enough variables have been taken into account. From the perspective of a relationship-driven approach, three of the most important reasons for avoiding black-and-white thinking are the following:

- *Almost all behaviors are on a spectrum* and not at the two (black or white) extremes. For example, we are virtually never entirely happy or entirely sad. Happy is one end of the spectrum, sad is at the opposite end, and we normally tend to fall somewhere in between. Recognizing the spectrum nature of behavior makes it much easier to accept approximations of appropriate behavior and to see positive movement toward the wanted behavior because we can see what is being done is further up the spectrum than the previous behavior. In contrast, black-and-white thinking allows us only two outcomes: success or failure.

- *Black-and-white thinking tends to ignore time and the fact that all things change over time.* We are not at all static creatures. We are never really the same twice. Skin has sloughed off and cells have died or regenerated while you are reading this. You have breathed in different molecules of air and exhaled others. You are now very slightly different than you were at the beginning of this sentence. Recognizing this continual process of change allows us to recognize the potential for things to be different than they are right now. In contrast, black-and-white thinking assumes permanence and looks for opportunities to reinforce that. Thus, once someone is in a category, the black-and-white thinker looks only for evidence that reinforces that category and ignores evidence of change, for example, "Once a bully, always a bully."

- *Black-and-white thinking does not take into account the nature of paradoxes,* also called dualism or levels in some quarters. To truly understand not only behavior but also how the world works in general, we need to be open to this concept of paradoxes, the idea that two apparently conflicting aspects are often operational at the same time in the same situation. There are many of these paradoxes that we all deal with every day. Objectivity versus subjectivity of perception is one example. We all, for instance, think subjectively by default (i.e., selfishly) from our own point of view. Children are born with this perspective, which undoubtedly has survival value. They need quality parenting in the early years to help them broaden their perspective to include others' points of view. Persons who primarily think subjectively will understand that tolerance, for example, should apply to *them;* however, if they are unable to think objectively, they will find it difficult to understand that tolerance should also apply to other people. They are usually only able to make this shift in perspective if there is something about the other person they can subjectively identify with (e.g., they can see how the person is like them). In order to develop genuine tolerance, this natural subjective perspective needs to be increasingly balanced with the ability to think objectively at the same time, to realize that while our perspective is true and legitimate for us, a different perspective may be just as true and legitimate for others. Consequently, we need to cultivate the ability to hold this paradox (that what we think subjectively is one valid reality while what is true objectively is another equally valid reality) in order to behave in a truly tolerant way.

Another paradox commonly encountered is free will versus fate or predetermination. In order to make successful changes, it is important to understand that we have free will, that we can *choose* to alter our lives effectively, and that ultimately we can gain a sense of control in almost every situation by learning to control our attitude. At the same time, however, we need an understanding of *fate*—the insight that there are always going to be circumstances beyond our control which will influence us. These factors include things like our genes, our environment, our personality type, our personal history, our socioeconomic status, our culture, our physical state and/or limitations, and so on, as well the *chaos factor*—that randomness in life that results in our being in the wrong place at the wrong time, or conversely, the right place at the right time for no apparent reason. Without the ability to hold this paradox, the black-and-white thinker tends to come down on one of the two extremes. If they favor the free-will extreme, then everything becomes cause/effect. We are responsible for everything that happens to us. If we make a mistake, have an accident, or get a horrible illness it is because we have not read the signs right, have not seen the right connections and, thus, not done the right things. If the black-and-white thinker favors the opposite extreme of fate or predetermination, then everything becomes the fault of someone or something else and a victim mentality occurs. Consequently, in order to make effective changes in our behavior, we need to accept the paradox that sometimes we're the pigeon, and sometimes we're the statue.

So it is important when working with a relationship-based methodology that one have a clear understanding that the world *is* complex, that we can't reduce it to clear-cut, comprehensible certainties, as dearly as we would all love to do so. This kind of open-ended acceptance can be difficult in a goal-oriented, assessment-based culture that is, by its very nature, reductionist; however, it remains one of the most crucial attributes for success in the dynamic realm of relationships.

4

Discipline

In describing an approach as flexible, responsive, and present oriented, it is easy to imagine that what results is simply an advanced form of *winging it*. No longer burdened with charts, contracts, point systems, and other methods that require extensive forward planning and recording, all the teacher has to do is appear in the classroom and wait for things to happen to which she can flexibly respond. This is not the case. Genuine flexibility, which allows us to make use of what is happening as it happens, comes not from hope-and-a-prayer chance taking but from the security of knowing there is an underlying foundation to what we do. Thus, we must first create this foundation. Before any children ever walk through the door, the teacher using relationships to change behavior needs to spend a good deal of time, thought, and energy laying the groundwork necessary to create the appropriate classroom milieu.

The biggest issue is inevitably discipline. The children already have a history of chaotic behavior, and the primary goal of placement in the classroom will be positive behavioral change. This will take precedence over all else, including academics. So it is crucial that the two main aspects of discipline—(1) establishing boundaries in order to make clear what is and what is not acceptable behavior and (2) what happens when unacceptable behavior occurs—are completely thought out, structured, and in place before the children arrive.

Just as it is easy to misunderstand flexibility as winging it, so too it is easy to misconstrue the relationship-driven approach's emphasis on tolerance as permissiveness and the idea that discipline requires no structured approach. It is essential to clear up this misconception straightaway.

Tolerance is not the same thing as permissiveness. Tolerance is understanding and accepting that a person is doing the best he can in a given situation at a given moment, even though that may fall well short of where he should be. Tolerance is understanding and accepting that things may look differently from another point of view. Tolerance is understanding and accepting that one's own perspective on things is necessarily limited by one's own self-oriented, subjective perspective, and the full, objective picture may be much different. So it is possible to be tolerant of a child who misbehaves without condoning the behavior while still upholding the need for change.

The relationship-driven methodology does not prejudge the child. The child is neutral (e.g., capable of both good and bad behavior), and the aim of the relationship-driven milieu is to respond flexibly to behavior as it happens with an aim to discouraging inappropriate behavior and encouraging appropriate behavior.

Permissiveness has a much different underlying belief structure. The child is regarded as a pure creature who instinctively knows best, whereas adults have become tainted by restrictions, misconceptions, and societal pressures to conform. Permissive methodology is child centered and child led. Structured discipline is eschewed in favor of using only positive interactions with children in an effort to allow their purity and creativity to remain intact or to reemerge. Adults are encouraged to approach children as friends and equals rather than as authorities.

In contrast, relationship-driven methodology operates from a humane perspective that recognizes tolerance, personal involvement, and compassion as important components of a successful teaching situation but also that the classroom is not a democracy. Of the 5, 10, 15, 50, or 500 individuals in any given class, the teacher has a unique role. To be designated the teacher signifies this person has maturity and experience that the students in the classroom do not have, and this brings with it special responsibilities. Among these responsibilities are

- caring for and protecting the students at all times, even when it means making unpopular decisions;
- providing an environment where everyone can prosper equally without fear of bullying, being left behind, or being left out;
- providing an environment which promotes learning;
- providing instruction; and
- providing adequate self-discipline skills/life skills to allow the student to continue moving forward after leaving the classroom.

In a classroom for behaviorally disordered children, the teacher's additional responsibility is to recognize that these students have been placed in this special environment because they have already demonstrated problems in self-control. So, while a time should come when these children are to contribute meaningfully to refining classroom rules, it is not appropriate that the children should determine what the boundaries are. This is the teacher's task.

So, the first and perhaps most important part of setting up a successful relationship-driven classroom is to establish ground rules or clear boundaries that will form the structure of the day-to-day operation of the classroom. This means deciding which rules and limits on behavior are necessary to bring about and keep order in the classroom and how these rules will be effectively enforced.

Why are clear boundaries so important at the onset of developing a relationship-driven classroom? The first reason for this is *safety*. Literal safety is obvious, so there is no need to detail that further. Equally important, however, is that clear boundaries also provide psychological safety. Because most children who come into behaviorally disordered classrooms have issues with self-control, they need the immediate sense of safety that clear ground rules provide. These communicate "Teacher is in control" but *not* control, as in "I'm bigger and stronger than you are, and so you have to follow my rules, because I will be able to make you follow them." This posture simply encourages power struggles, casting the teacher into role of prison warden and feeding into cycles with which the child is most likely already familiar. Instead, we are endeavoring to communicate "I am in control of myself and my environment. This means I am strong and safe, and I will be able to successfully keep you safe." One of the foremost ways a healthy, functional adult keeps a child safe is by providing clear, consistent limits on the child's behavior so that he or she does not hurt him- or herself or others.

The second reason for establishing ground rules at the onset is *consistency.* Most children who come into behaviorally disordered classrooms have experienced inconsistent behavior from adults in response to their actions. Unpredictable responses lead to anxiety and uncertainty about how adults behave. Unpredictable behavior also tends to strengthen inappropriate behavior due to the power of intermittent reinforcement, and it encourages the development of manipulative behavior designed to exploit the inconsistency. Clear ground rules communicate "Teacher is predictable in how he will respond when I misbehave," which lays the foundation for "Teacher is trustworthy, because I know how he will respond."

The third reason for establishing ground rules at the onset is *caring.* Many children who come into behaviorally disordered classrooms do not have much experience of healthy, consistent, and caring relationships with adults. Much misbehavior occurs because it is the only behavior guaranteed to garner adult attention. Other misbehavior results from the child having learned to exploit situations before he himself is exploited. And some misbehavior happens simply because no one has bothered to teach the child otherwise. Clear, consistently applied ground rules communicate "I care how you act."

There is no single magic set of ground rules for a relationship-driven classroom because each teacher and her classroom are unique. The setting up of rules should be sufficiently flexible to allow for the school district's legal and ethical requirements, the teacher's individual temperament, tastes, and peeves, plus the physical constraints of the classroom layout, such as size, adult-to-child ratio, and so on. The following, however, we find is a useful guideline in devising ground rules.

Make the rules simple and easily communicated. In *One Child,* Torey's classroom famously had only two ground rules:

1. Do your best work.

2. You are not allowed to hurt people, animals, or things that belong to others or are for everyone to use.

These rules were easily comprehended by all the children and easily remembered and repeated. Be positive in stating the rules, if you can, as it is often helpful for the children to know what they are expected *to do,* as opposed to only what they are not to do, but don't get hung up on semantics. Clarity is more important, and sometimes negative statements work better simply because they are more easily understood. Language is, at the end of the day, just language, and its whole point is communication. So if "Don't spit" is clearer than "Please keep your saliva in your mouth," then opt for that.

KEEP THE RULES OPEN-ENDED AND FLEXIBLE

One of the problems with methodologies that focus on control is their tendency to produce a plethora of black-and-white rules. At first glance, this looks like a good thing that clear-cut, unambiguous rules are a good choice. Our experience, however, is that out in the real world this is often not the case. The first problem with such rules is the potential for power struggles. Difficult, defiant children often react to black-and-white rules as if the teacher had drawn the proverbial line in the dirt and said, "Don't cross this." The kid's just got to break that rule to prove he or she can. This puts the teacher into the difficult position of either having to escalate to confrontation or risk losing authority or consistency by ignoring the rule breaker. This is an undesirable situation because the teacher is being forced to react to the student rather than respond, and this is never a position of strength. So it works better if the rules are flexible enough to allow for face-saving behavior and to allow reasonable amounts of testing behavior to be ignored, when this is situationally appropriate.

The second problem with black-and-white rules is that we humans are messy creatures living in a messy world. Life itself is never black-and-white. There are times when one must respond with utter consistency, but there are also times when extenuating circumstances mean that rules need to be ignored, bent, or even broken in order to get the most out of the moment. Open-ended rules allow one to do this more easily without undermining authority.

Of the rules used in the *One Child* classroom, "Do your best," is an example of an open-ended, flexible rule which is clear to the child (most children *do* have a sense of when they are trying hard), and yet it allows both the teacher and the child some wiggle room in interpreting and applying the rule. "Do your best" allowed Torey to acknowledge that on a particularly difficult day, half an assignment probably *was* the child's best, even though normally the child would be expected to finish it. The second rule "You are not allowed to hurt people, animals or things that belong to others or are for everyone to use" is more specific, which is important when we are dealing with safety issues, but it still allows for flexible interpretation in instances of accidental behavior and in terms of what constitutes "things for everyone to use."

ADD RULES AS YOU NEED THEM

Classroom rules are not stone tablets handed down from God. While it is important to have ground rules when you start and to know clearly what they are, they *can* be changed, amended, and added to, if necessary. Our experience is that it is best to start with as few rules as possible, which are flexible to inter-pretation and which cover things broadly, and then add more or clarify as one goes along and discovers places where rules aren't working. This prevents the children from being over-whelmed at the start of class by a long list of rules and avoids giving the impression that Teacher is a control freak. It also allows for customization from group to group, because not every class is going to have the same kinds of problems.

As the year wore on, Torey often had two sets of rules going in her classroom. The first were hers that were in place from the beginning of the year and established the absolute boundar-ies for the group. However, she also often had a second list of Our Rules, which the kids helped create as they went along. If, for instance, they had a specific, intractable problem, they discussed it in class circle, decided what the rule should be and what the consequences should be, and added it to the list of Our Rules that she displayed along with her rules. These often tended to be pedantic and specific, such as "Don't spit in peo-ple's lunches," but as they addressed specific, germane prob-lems that were upsetting the children, the new rules were often helpful. And of course, on those occasions when the rule was too pedantic or just plain didn't work, this could prove a useful exercise for the children in how to adjust limits. Do keep these kid-created rules separate from the ground rules, however, as the latter are the grown-up rules made from your maturity, experience, and authority as an adult.

DISPLAY THE RULES PROMINENTLY

This gives them importance and legitimacy. It doesn't mat-ter if the children can't read (although obviously the teacher wants to be sure the children understand what is written). Displaying them isn't about needing to refer to them; it's about making them public and important. Displaying them also makes them more objective. What gives power struggles their potency is that they are personal; they are one person pitted again another person, each trying to get the better of the other. "The rule on the board says . . ." can help defuse this simply because it is less personal than "I say . . ."

Devising rules that are fair, flexible, and workable provides the framework of the relationship-driven milieu, but the engine that drives it is found in what happens when these rules are broken. The most crucial part of planning for a relationship-driven classroom is how do we respond when misbehavior happens?

In a relationship-driven classroom, consequences are not the only appropriate response to discipline and control. We know this sounds strange. We have become so accustomed to the idea of the A-B-C chain from science-based methodologies and from the cause/effect accountability of market-based methodologies that we often fail to consider that there even are other possibilities. We think automatically "If kids misbehave, then, of course, there must be consequences. That's the only way to *get* them to behave." Not only do we fail to think outside the box on this one; we also often fail to realize whether there even *is* a box or dogma or opinion that could be thought outside of. The actual fact is that consequences are only one of the possible responses we can make to misbehavior. Sometimes they are the best response. Sometimes they aren't.

Here, now, is the most important thing we are going to say in this entire book. If you want to skip everything else, here is the digested read: *Never forget you are a teacher.* Being a teacher overarches every other aspect of what you do. That's what you trained to be. That's what the school board employed you to be. That's why the children come to you. You are not a prison warden. You are not a psychologist. You are not a research scientist. You are a teacher. Your job—and, we hope, your gift—is to teach. This means you want to approach *every* situation in the classroom with a mind open to teaching opportunities, because this is what you are there to do.

From this point on we will often refer to *active or actively teaching* or *direct* or *directly teaching*. This simply means doing what you were trained to do (e.g., identify a topic, determine an appropriate means of delivering it, make lesson plans and gather materials where necessary, and then directly teach it). This is as opposed to teaching by indirect or intuitive methods, such as modeling or assuming knowledge will be absorbed by osmosis.

A gigantic amount of misbehavior occurs because the child simply does not know how to behave differently, because she has misconceptions about how she should behave, or because she has misconceptions about herself. These situations are not corrective occasions. They are teaching opportunities. They are chances to permanently change misbehavior by teaching the child how to behave differently. Consequences are often quite inefficient at this, so we want a wider repertoire.

To clarify, an example of a child who misbehaves because he does not know how to behave differently was 6-year-old Sheila in *One Child*. Sheila was often very rude to the other children, taking things away from them without asking, pushing in front of them, ignoring them when they were helpful to her, and so forth. The natural consequence of this was that other children didn't like her very well and didn't want to play with her. Using a behavioral model, a logical positive consequence would have been to set up a star chart and give her a star each time she remembered to ask first before taking something. A logical negative consequence would have been a few minutes' time-out for taking things from others without asking. All of these would, through trial and error, eventually teach Sheila that politeness is something she needs to conform to in the classroom, although she still may not recognize it as an important social skill. It was more efficient, however, to regard Sheila's behavior as a teaching opportunity. She didn't actually know *how* to be polite (*didn't know how to behave differently*). *Please* and *thank you* were not used regularly in her home environment, and she had not been actively taught social skills by the adults around her. So role-playing and direct teaching were used (When you want something, you say, "Please may I have it," and if they give it to you, you say, "Thank you."), and when she forgot, she was reminded. Natural consequences in the form of the other children responding more positively to her efforts to be polite reinforced this teaching.

There is often a marked prejudice against the idea that children are misbehaving because they do not know how to behave differently. People will react with "Well, he *should* know," and the implication is that the behavior ought to have been absorbed without being actively taught, simply because a child has reached a given age. Using the example above regarding politeness, it is common to assume that because the teacher is polite and uses *please* and *thank you* to the child, the child should automatically learn this. Consequently, the child who persists with rude behavior is perceived as willfully choosing that behavior. Our experience is that this is usually not true. While some observant, socially astute children will indeed mimic adult behavior and pick up desirable behaviors in this way, the majority of children, particularly those with emotional issues clouding their internal environment, need the adults around them to focus on the behavior and actively teach what is appropriate. To be intolerant of their need to be taught is neither helpful nor appropriate.

A child who has misconceptions about how he should behave can be illustrated by 6-year-old Robert. He persistently used aggressive, inappropriate talk, and swearing. Robert was living in a household comprised of his mother, her sisters, and her parents. Robert's grandparents argued frequently. His grandfather drank heavily and when drunk was physically and verbally abusive toward his wife and daughters. Robert had regularly witnessed his family's aggressive verbal behavior and had no other models of male behavior except his grandfather. Consequently, he was under the misconception that when interacting with others, using aggressive language was appropriate because this was how it was done in his environment. Again, using a behavioral model, a logical positive consequence would have been to set up a token system whereby he earned tokens for managing to go X amount of time without this kind of talk. A logical negative consequence would have been to take away a token every time he swore.

And again, this would potentially control the problem while Robert was in the token economy. However, it was more helpful to regard Robert's behavior as a teaching opportunity. He was behaving in a way that *was* appropriate in his own environment, and he needed help understanding that in the wider world a different kind of behavior is used. Role-play was used to teach more appropriate responses, and then he was reminded of what these were if he slipped up.

Misconceptions about how to behave are rather like inadvertently speaking a foreign language. You give what you think is an acceptable response, but no one around you takes it that way. If you are rewarded every time you say "good" and punished every time you say "*bon*," you will eventually learn to say "good" and avoid saying "*bon*" through trial and error, but this will not teach you why. The *meaning* of the change is likely to remain superficial (i.e., good/*bon* are related to gaining a reward or avoiding punishment) instead of clarifying the real issue: What was appropriate in another environment doesn't work in this environment. As a consequence, you are less likely to generalize the change to other areas and more likely to revert to what is familiar to you when the reward/punishment isn't present. A more effective method would be for someone to teach the appropriate response (in this environment you need to speak English, because that is what people here understand, and the English word is "good"). This is more efficient than trial and error learning and will usually have a longer lasting impact.

Again, Sheila from *One Child* is a good example of a child who misbehaves because of misconceptions about herself. Sheila repeatedly destroyed schoolwork and usually refused to take part in seatwork. The natural consequence of this was that very little assessment had been done, and thus, no one knew which skills she had and which were lacking. Logical consequences for her behavior included time-out for destroying the work, repeatedly replacing destroyed work until she did it, and rewarding her for sitting down with her work. These controlled the problem externally but did not generalize to other settings.

However, in developing a relationship with Sheila, it became clear that her misconception of herself as a bad girl and as a failure underpinned her refusal to do seatwork and her inability to complete work that had been started. Helping to establish more appropriate perceptions by teaching accurate self-assessment and encouraging efforts to live up to these more accurate assessments resolved this problem entirely.

So discipline in a relationship-driven classroom can be summed up as never pass up an opportunity to teach.

CONSEQUENCES

Understanding misbehavior as a lack of awareness of or as a lack of skills necessary for more productive behavior is a vital concept in dealing with rule breaking. Subsequently, many incidents can be handled with reminders, direct teaching, or acceptance of approximations. Nonetheless, there are times when consequences are the best way forward.

In using consequences to deal with misbehavior in a relationship-driven classroom, it is helpful to know what consequences are available to you from the outset, to start small with the least punishment likely to get the job done, to use natural consequences when feasible and safe to do so, and to avoid vindictive consequences.

Know What Consequences Are Available to You From the Outset

This may seem obvious, but it is surprising how often we get ourselves into the situation first and then have to think how to counter the resultant misbehavior. This tends to lead to reacting rather than responding. It also tends to decrease teacher flexibility. What kinds of consequences are you comfortable with and able to implement immediately when needed? Stern voice? Evil eye? Warning system? Time-out? Loss of privileges?

Start Small

This isn't shock-and-awe territory. Many people operate under the mistaken belief that if they respond strongly to a misbehavior the first time around that is more likely to stop it in its tracks. In fact, this is seldom true. Too strong a response only produces unhelpful emotional side effects. The child becomes frightened or angry, and these emotions then sabotage his efforts to adopt a more appropriate behavior. Moreover, too strong a response does not model the kind of appropriate behavior you want the children to learn. You are *always* the model in the classroom, so it's important to behave as you want them to behave. Too strong a response sends the message that might makes right. In addition, too strong a response encourages power struggles and with this, the need to save face because the stakes are high. Finally, too strong an initial response makes it difficult to escalate to a stronger response, if needed, because you are already near the top of your range.

Always begin with the least consequence you can get away with and then reapply, if necessary. For instance, start with 5 minutes in the quiet chair for a fighting child to get control of herself, not 20. If, after 5 minutes she isn't in control, then another 5 minutes. Only escalate to 10 minutes if it is obvious she is nowhere near control at the end of 5.

✏ Use Natural Consequences When Feasible and Safe to Do So

Natural consequences occur automatically as the naturally occurring result of a particular behavior. If a student constantly complains about his peers, a natural consequence is that he isn't chosen when the class plays during recess. If a student lies, a natural consequence is that the student's peers don't believe her. Natural consequences are generally better because they are more objective than arbitrary consequences like time-out. This makes them come across to the child as more impartial. Equally important, because they are the consequences nature hands out, the child will encounter them in the real world. Not only is it helpful to align the order in the classroom with the real world, but it is also helpful to teach children the connection between their actions and natural consequences in preparation for a safe and successful life.

Avoid Vindictive Consequences

If a child's misbehavior is upsetting, it is easy to react with consequences which are, ultimately, an expression of our angry or hurt feelings. In *One Child* Torey was absent from the classroom for 2 days and Sheila, who had been doing very well at that point, just lost it and became very destructive. When Torey returned and discovered all the damage, she felt very angry and even more so, very disappointed in Sheila, and she denied her the privilege of going on a field trip. This is an example of vindictive consequences. Torey was personally upset, and she hit back in a way she knew would hurt. It's understandable, but it's inappropriate. Appropriate consequences occurred at the time the damage took place and were related to what happened. Sheila had to replace all the books she pulled out of the book cases and the stuff she pulled off the walls. It is easier to avoid vindictive consequences if we are aware right from the start that we are vulnerable to them and if we already have a decent arsenal of appropriate consequences available for use.

Sometimes it is difficult to tell the difference between vindictive consequences and natural consequences. Natural consequences can sometimes be harsh or longer lasting than arbitrary consequences for the same level of behavior, but they still may be appropriate. For example, Torey had one boy, Fred, who always dawdled when putting on or taking off his outer clothes, and she found herself continually nagging him to hurry up. So she opted for natural consequences. She told him that the bus would be there in 5 minutes, and he needed to be dressed. He wasn't, so the bus left, and Fred had to wait at school until someone could come collect him, which upset him

very much. This was a longer lasting and more severe consequence for his dawdling than she would have given, but it was
connected to his behavior in a straightforward, natural way
that Fred could immediately grasp and remember.

Be Open to Approximation

Approximation is what we do when we are learning a new
behavior. It usually takes several efforts or *approximations* before
a new behavior actually comes together, because all behaviors
require that a set of actions occur in the right sequence. To master this requires memory of the task, understanding of how it
goes together, and practice. It would be quite inappropriate, for
example, for us to expect to be able to pick up a violin and play
a sonata perfectly if we had never done it before, even if we'd
seen many other people do it many other times. Playing a new
piece of music perfectly would be difficult for an accomplished
violinist. It would be impossible for someone who had never
touched a violin previously. So a period of approximation is
required, a time when we get our head around what is required
and then practice the piece of music, and eventually we will
come closer and closer to being able to play it well.

The same holds true for all behaviors, including those in the
classroom. A child may genuinely want to change his behavior,
but because he is not yet adept, he initially falls short of the
desired behavior. It is important to recognize and encourage
these approximations for what they are, rather than regarding
them as failures to complete the behavior perfectly.

For example, Billy in *Beautiful Child* had a tendency to
swear excessively and a goal was set to change this. The first
step—the first level of approximation of the desired behavior
(no swearing)—is awareness. Billy showed this by emitting
the swear word but then clamping his hand over his mouth
saying, "Oops." He was still saying the swear word, so this
was not the desired behavior, but it was important to recognize
that this was an approximation of the desired behavior rather
than misbehavior. His next level of approximation was to

catch himself after he had started the word but before he had finished it. This usually resulted in his clamping his hand over his mouth as he was saying, "Fffff—." His next level of approximation involved starting to say the word but not clamping his hand over his mouth. He simply paused and then changed it to something appropriate, as in "Fffff—fiddle!"

It is very important the teacher be on the lookout for approximations and to reinforce them. This reassures the child she is on the right path, but also that someone notices she is trying and that it matters. There may still be consequences, if the inappropriate behavior actually occurs. In Billy's instance, he was being *fined* tokens for swearing, and he still lost a token if he actually swore. It's crucial, however, to pair the consequence with positive reinforcement of the approximation. In Billy's instance, this meant verbally praising him for his effort to control the word and reassurance that next time he would no doubt succeed. This puts the child and the teacher on the same team against the behavior, and this is your goal. Throughout the entire paradigm of the relationship-driven model, this is your goal. You and the kid are on one team against the behavior. It is never you on one team against the kid and his behavior.

ADDITIONAL GUIDELINES FOR SUCCESSFUL CLASSROOM MANAGEMENT

Here are a few extra thoughts about what goes into the successful management of classroom problems.

Recognize That the Child Is Not Able to Be His or Her Own Teacher

This, to us, is the most fundamental rule of discipline. A lot of problems arise from the fact the child does not know how to behave differently. Yes, he has been told a million times before. Yes, he *should* know. But he's still doing it, so clearly he *doesn't* know. Not really. We're back to this whole concept of *no one chooses to be unhappy*. If he is making a mess of his life, if he is unhappy and making everyone else unhappy, you can pretty much rest assured it isn't because he woke up that morning thinking, "Wow, I want to have a crap time today." Nobody thinks like that. So if he's doing stuff to give himself (and you, in the process) a really crap day, then it is because he simply doesn't have a different way of behaving securely in his repertoire. He is reverting to old, unsuccessful behaviors because while they are ineffective, they are familiar, and he knows how to do them. We are at our hearts, all of us, creatures of habit. So when this happens, *this is a teaching opportunity*. It is, however, unrealistic to expect him to teach himself. If he were capable of that, he would have done it before now and avoided this crap day. So, it is a teaching opportunity *for you*. He is not able to come up with more successful behaviors on his own and/ or put them in place. You are the teacher. Your responsibility in the classroom is to teach the students, and discipline is just one more subject. Tackle it as if it were math. When a child misbehaves, think, "What doesn't he know about this situation? What are the component parts? How can it be broken down so that he understands how it goes together and can learn it?" And then support him as he approximates the correct behavior.

Aim for Responsibility, Not Obedience

Obedience puts discipline into an external context. In other words, the child perceives it as "I'm doing what I'm supposed to because you will punish me, if I don't." The punisher is controlling the child's behavior, not the child herself. We want to change this to where the child internalizes this control herself by becoming responsible for her own behavior. "I'm doing what I'm supposed to because that's how people in this classroom act, and I'm a member of this classroom."

Become Aware of the Principles of Moral Development

Responsibility is classed as part of our moral character. To aid children in achieving responsibility for their behavior instead of simply obedience, it is helpful to have a working knowledge of how morality develops, because people cannot *jump* moral stages. Instead, we progress developmentally through moral stages much the same as we progress through cognitive developmental stages. Understanding these stages ensures we do not have unrealistic expectations of what a child can do.

Lawrence Kohlberg (1981) provides one of the best studies on the matter and has identified six stages of development that fall into three categories:

1. *Preconventional morality:* There are two stages at this level of moral thinking that begin to develop in toddlerhood. In Stage 1, the child's thinking is very black-and-white. He perceives *good* as a fixed set of rules handed down by powerful authorities that must be followed. Toddlers see morality as external to themselves, as that which authorities tell them they must do and punishment is why disobedience is *bad*. In Stage 2, the child begins to recognize that there is not just one right view. Different people have different views and the *right view* can be relative. Thus, each person behaves according to self-interest (what is right for him or her), and punishment is simply an *occupational hazard* of having a different view from someone else of what is right. This is a fairly amoral stage, except for the burgeoning sense of connectedness to others that comes in the form of *fair deals* of the "if you scratch my back, I'll scratch yours" type. These two levels are called preconventional because the children do not take into account anyone except themselves. There is no sense of being a member of society.

   Most children in classes for behavior disorders will be operating at one of these two levels. Our goal in the relationship-driven classroom is to encourage them toward the next level.

2. *Conventional morality:* Again, there are two stages at this level. By Stage 3, children begin to understand morality is more than doing what is good for oneself. They begin to believe people should live up to expectations of their family, their community, and their country. Being good means having good motives and positive feelings for

others, such as love, trust, and concern for others. This is the period of *best friends* and really wanting to get to know other people and their feelings and needs. At Stage 4, the individual becomes more conscious of society as a whole. Good motives are no longer enough. Good behavior is now seen as not only having the right intention but also maintaining order in society. There is a new respect for authority and for law and order, making this stage look superficially the same as Stage 1, but a little probing makes it clear that obedience at this stage is based on a concept of the *good of everyone* as opposed to avoidance of punishment.

3. *Postconventional morality:* At Stage 4, people perceive a well-run society as a good one, but organization alone does not ensure that a society is moral. As they reach Stage 5, people begin to be able to think about society in an abstract way. They understand that different people have different perspectives, but they believe all *good people* would agree on two points: One, that there are basic human rights that apply to everyone, and these should be protected; and two, that there should be a democratic process (e.g., everyone should have a voice) for changing rules and/or improving society. Stage 6, which is very rarely reached, is the point where people begin to follow what are called universal principles. There are certain universal principles that underline all the major religions: goodness, rightness, mercy, compassion, and things of this sort. The individual behaves morally out of genuine compassion with no payback to himself. He simply perceives that this is the right way to live.

Let Group Control Provide Part of the Discipline

Group behavior is an excellent medium for discipline, particularly when the entire class is involved. The opening or closing circle makes a good venue for raising group issues and letting the group discuss how to deal with problems. It is valuable sometimes, however, to stop the children right where they are and say, "OK, here's the problem. How are we going to solve it?" Once the group identity is strong, this works even if the problem involves only a couple of children, as long as it can be done in a calm, nonaggressive manner so that the problem causers do not feel picked on.

Occasionally use group identity as a corrective tool. This needs to be done with a light hand and always phrased in a way that includes the child as part of the group, not excludes him. For example, we *don't* say, "No chipmunk would act like you have!" Instead, phrase it as "You're a chipmunk. How do chipmunks treat others' property, disagree with someone, something, and so on?"

Also, occasionally treat them as a group rather than individuals and make the group responsible for controlling *wanderers*. This removes you entirely from the control seat and provides a good opportunity for students to learn how to control others without bullying. It also encourages self-control.

Punishment

We are not adverse to punishment being part of the disciplinary canon. There are definitely times when punishment is the most effective and appropriate response. What we need to keep in mind, however, is that punishment is the poorest teacher, because it is very inflexible. It teaches only obedience and this it teaches only through fear of consequences. Our ultimate goal is to teach responsibility. So if the opportunity to teach responsibility is available in a given situation, it's best to choose that alternative.

When you do need to use punishment, keep the following in mind:

- *Know before you start what your consequences are* and make these clear to the child at the onset. It may be a quiet chair or a naughty step. It may be loss of classroom privileges. It may reflect your own school's policies. It may simply be that you will sit down with the child yourself and make sure a very thorough job is done of the task.

Whatever, know ahead of time what it will be, and inform the child at the start. This differentiates it from a threat.

- *Start small and work up.* Control models tend to start with big consequences with the idea of achieving obedience quickly. Hence, we see shock-and-awe tactics often used when we want to control. The relationship-driven methodology is a teaching model, not a control model. We work on approximation. So we start with the smallest punishment likely to get the job done. This gives us a next step if we need to escalate. It deters power struggles and humiliating a *loser.* Most importantly, it does the least damage to the teaching milieu.

- *Don't threaten; remind.* Threats are a hugely ineffective control method, so don't say anything you don't intend to back up with action. Instead of "If you get out of your seat one more time, I'm sending you to time-out," issue reminders such as "Remember, we're supposed to be sitting in our seats, watching a film now."

- *Limit the number of reminders.* Torey operated under the adage once a mistake, twice a mistake, three times a fool. The children were given two reminders about their behavior, and if they didn't sort themselves out, the third time meant a consequence. Decide on a policy for this. Let the children know what it is. Then follow through, otherwise reminders become as empty of meaning as threats. This isn't the moment for managing without consequences. Managing without consequences is only effective if you have not already started down the path of consequences. Be consistent.

- *Always follow up a punishment with a chat* once the child has calmed down. There are six important reasons for this:

  1. You need to ascertain that the child actually understood which behavior got her into trouble. Kids can get remarkably confused about this, or, if they are in a state of high emotion when they were sent to the quiet

chair or whatever, it can often just be a blur to them about what happened. Make sure they know and can say it back to you.

2. Follow up provides a chance for the child to verbalize alternative behaviors for the next time this situation occurs. Again, make sure he can say these alternatives back to you. Don't do all the talking yourself.

3. The situation may need fixing. If there has been some kind of fallout as a result of the child's actions, such as someone being hurt or something being broken or ruined, ask the child what she thinks can be done to ameliorate the situation. Help her out by saying, "How would you feel if that happened to you," and so on, but don't put words in her mouth. Let the child draw her own conclusions as best she can and give suggestions at this stage if she is stuck.

4. Reassure the child directly or indirectly that you still like him and are glad to have him returning to the class. This is important. Many children come from backgrounds where punishment is tied up with rejection, hostility, or disinterest. Reassure the child that you can distinguish between him and the act and that you are confident he is capable of doing the right thing.

5. You can assess whether the child is actually ready to leave the quiet chair. If she isn't able to answer these questions fairly and straightforwardly, it's likely the behavior will quickly repeat.

6. This chat is not meant to be a psychological deconstruction. Once children are used to the format, it shouldn't take more than a couple of minutes to go through these six points, and it is helpful to make this clear as well, or else *talkers* will take advantage of it to argue their point. If you need more than a few minutes with a child, schedule it separately. This not only

allows you to get back to the class, but it gives the miscreant time to cool down.

Actively Teach Self-Management

Finally, it is important to give children themselves the tools of self-management. We often get caught up in a perverse cycle of unrealistic expectations where we focus on and punish negative behaviors while failing to teach the appropriate, positive behaviors with which we want the children to replace these negative behaviors, because we imagine the children know what they are and how to achieve them.

Ways of teaching self-management include the following:

- *Group discussion.* This is one of the best methods for identifying appropriate behaviors and troubleshooting self-management techniques. It can be done as part of problem-solving discussions, but it also works well as part of daily circle. Bring up general issues as scenarios, such as getting angry, feeling embarrassed, or being frightened, and allow the group to discuss how they could handle the situation. For example, you could present a scenario such as "James is in line for lunch when the boy behind him bumps James's tray and makes his drink spill. How does James handle that?" First, help the group see that there may be several different reasons why this happened. Second, help the group sympathize with James but at the same time understand that it is important James not make the situation worse. Third, discuss ways James can manage his feelings and manage this problem.
- *Actively teach about emotions.* This is a hugely critical area because emotional reaction is almost always at the root of misbehavior. Children need to develop awareness of their emotions before they can manage control of them. Children also need to know that emotions *can* be controlled and that there are actually very quick, automatic thoughts happening before the emotion happens. One

of the best ways of showing this is to talk about why, for example, a baby isn't frightened when you point a gun at it but someone older would be. The baby doesn't have enough life experience to *think* of the gun as dangerous. In a similar way, we can become very frightened if someone points a gun at us, but then the gun turns out to be a toy. We experienced fear because we *thought* it was real. These thoughts are extremely fast, so fast that all we are really aware of experiencing is the fear. But the thoughts do still happen, and it's those thoughts we need to tap into to stop the emotions that follow them. Children often find this insight both fascinating and incredible. In terms of learning self-management, it is very important they become familiar with it.

- *Actively teach emotional control.* There are many techniques for getting control of emotions. Talking about them and practicing them helps the child approximate them. Some examples include the following:
  - o *Withdrawing from a potential flash point.* Teach the concept of "discretion is the better part of valor. Help children learn to recognize when things are getting out of hand, both by internal sensations/tensions and by clues and to understand walking away from a conflict at this point is not cowardice.
  - o *Time-out.* Teach how the idea of time-out is not about punishment but rather taking ourselves out of situations where we are not in control and giving ourselves a bit of peace to collect our thoughts and feelings. Teach the concept of counting to 10 or of going out of the room/to somewhere else as a means of controlling temper. Assist them in understanding that even with situations that need to be resolved, it is more helpful to wait until everyone is calm, so sometimes it works better to take a break and come back to the problem later.
  - o *Diversion.* Strong emotions can often be handled by diverting them into more appropriate physical expression, such as exercise, punching pillows, or

even singing or dancing. Sometimes we can divert our anger or other strong emotions into something more useful. It can become a spur for change or to get helpful things accomplished.

o *The other point of view.* Learning to switch thinking to the other point of view is an effective way of bringing emotions under control because it loosens up that subjective grasp we have on the situation and reestablishes a sense of connection with others. This takes practice, which is why it should be a vital component of any teaching of self-management, but it is invaluable in defusing me-versus-them.

- *Using I-messages.* Learning to express concerns with I-messages ("I haven't got as many") rather than the accusatory you-messages ("You aren't giving me my share") tends to allow for better communication and results in less emotionally provocative situations.

- *Relaxation exercises.* Meditation, relaxing music, and other relaxation techniques all contribute to better managed emotions.

- *Journaling or other communication forms.* One of the great challenges is teaching children the difference between letting go of strong emotions and suppressing them. This is particularly true with anger. Journaling is one of the most effective ways of teaching this, as it allows the child to express her strong feelings but in a way that is generally easier to let go of once they are expressed. Traditional journals work well, but it doesn't need to be this formal to be effective. Encourage children to write down their feelings any time they are so explosive as to need intervention. The child does not need to write particularly well or expansively for this to be successful, as long as there is no sense of judgment about the quality. If the child doesn't write, have him or her draw pictures. Do use it as a communication, especially in the beginning when the child is establishing the skill, which means do respond to their efforts. Either write a note back or talk with the child. Other expressive arts can also be used here, but as a quick self-management tool, writing remains the easiest.

- *Actively reinforce positive efforts at self-management.* This is a difficult skill for all of us, but it is especially challenging for impulsive or distractible children; so it is important to help them identify when they are getting it right. Acknowledge approximations as well as successful behaviors.

- *Encourage the whole group to reinforce each other's efforts at self-management.* This raises consciousness among the children for each other doing these kinds of things, which is helpful in itself, and it encourages children to see situations from others' points of view. It also tends to have a positive effect on self-esteem when peers reinforce behavior. One of the best tools for this is the Kobold's Box.

- Finally, *when in one-to-one conversation with children, encourage them to self-assess in this area.* Ask them how they feel they are doing managing their behavior, what they feel are weak areas, and help them troubleshoot. Learning to accurately self-assess is one of the key components to self-management.

5

Creating a Positive Classroom Climate

I n our experience, the reason control-oriented methodologies are often unsuccessful in the classroom is because the focus is on obedience rather than change. The ultimate goal of these methodologies is compliance with a predetermined, external standard imposed by those in authority. Accountability is measured by the number of students who meet this standard at a given time.

The ultimate goal of a relationship-driven methodology is change. Obedience, while preferable to misbehavior, is of limited value in the long term because it is externally governed. If the external authority is not present, oftentimes the desired behavior is no longer present either. The only way to ensure a desired behavior remains in place once the child is outside the controlled classroom environment is if change has genuinely occurred within the individual. So in structuring a relationship-driven classroom, it is important that it be a place that encourages change to happen rather than obedience.

In our experience, change requires these components:

- *Freedom to approximate.* As mentioned previously, when we are learning something new, we are not perfect at it in the beginning. So in order for change to take place, we need room to try out the new behavior, secure that our effort will be recognized as trying, and support and reassurance that we are moving in the right direction, even if we are currently not succeeding.
- *Freedom to experiment (practice trial-and-error learning).* Humans learn better first hand. We remain more interested and more engaged in processes over which we have some control and the opportunity to experiment. Experiencing the natural consequences of trial and error often provides meaningful motivation to persevere with change.
- *Freedom to fail.* Not all our efforts at change will be successful. This does not mean, however, they are invalid, wrong, or useless. Indeed, quite often we learn far more from our failures than our successes, but this only happens in a climate where failure is not a major source of humiliation, distress, or punishment.
- *Opportunities for social interaction.* Other people matter. We innately want to belong, to be esteemed, and to be loved. We learn a huge amount from other human beings. We imitate them, we model ourselves on them, and we endeavor to integrate with them. We also use others as a continual yardstick by which to judge ourselves.
- *Opportunities for creativity.* The whole concept of change depends heavily on the ability of the child to adapt from her old behavior to the new one. Creativity encourages flexibility both in adapting the change to the child and the child to the change, but it also helps to *loosen up* the child's (and our) thinking. Many problems in behavior management are due more to the perception that things are fixed and permanent and can't be different than they actually are. On a more personal scale, things become

our own when we are able to interact creatively with them. This holds true whether it is a concrete item, such as a piece of paper, or an abstract concept, such as how to behave courteously. To fully integrate a desired change, a child must become confident enough about it to play with it, to experiment with it, and to personalize it.

- *Reasonable freedom from punishment.* Because learning to do something differently inevitably involves failure and backsliding as part of the natural process, it is important that any environment designed to encourage change also guarantees a reasonable amount of freedom from punishment. There are times when punishment is appropriate and when it is a healthy part of the learning experience, but it needs to be the exception, not the rule. Punishment is a form of external control whereas personal change involves developing internal control. For genuine change to take place, the child needs the opportunity to interact, approximate, experiment, and occasionally fail without punishment as the only response.

When creating a relationship-driven classroom, the obvious goal is to build a positive environment in which change can take place. So what practical steps can be taken when planning such a classroom?

BUILD IN A STRUCTURED ROUTINE

A well-planned daily classroom routine is the backbone of a successful relationship-driven classroom. At first glance, advice to create a structured routine appears to counter all the previous talk about flexibility, but it is important to remember that a relationship-driven model is not a permissive model. Permissiveness is allowing people to do what they want when they want. To children whose lives are already in chaos, permissiveness will make them feel unsafe. It is crucial to understand that an environment first must meet our basic need for safety and security before it can give rise to learning, growth, flexibility, and spontaneity. Flexibility and spontaneity without structure in place first are just other names for disorganization.

On the other hand, having a structured routine in a relationship-driven classroom is also not selling out to the *curriculum of control* ethos. The highly structured routines of such methodologies as token economies, for example, are structured with the sole intention of controlling behavior and evoking obedience. In the relationship-driven classroom, structure is there not to control but rather to promote a sense of safety and to bring organization to thoughts and actions.

So, we are looking to create a classroom with a structured routine because

- *it provides a more secure atmosphere and lessens anxiety.* Most children in classes for behavioral problems will come from chaotic, erratic backgrounds with low levels of consistency. This confusing environment will have contributed significantly to their difficulties, so the establishment of a structured routine right from the onset helps the child settle in more quickly and is often enough on its own to calm many lesser behavioral problems.
- *it provides order.* Most children in these classes are chaotic thinkers and have difficulty following directions, making changes, and focusing their attention. An orderly routine helps them minimize these difficulties.
- *it provides a level of inherent discipline.* In a structured environment, boundaries are clearer, and unpredictable triggers occur less commonly.
- *it teaches organizational skills and forward thinking.* We learn what we live.
- *it provides maintenance of the teaching program in the teacher's absence.* Substitutes, aides, auxiliaries, volunteer classroom helpers, and parents have a better chance of maintaining the teacher's program in her absence. She will be away, whether through illness, professional training, or

unforeseen events. It's inevitable. With a good structured routine, it is much easier for others to carry on without causing upset or damage to the children.

BUILD IN OPPORTUNITIES FOR JOY AND ENTHUSIASM

Enthusiasm is an expression of one's delight at being in a situation and it is both contagious and a powerful but vastly underrated motivator. By building opportunities for enthusiasm into your curriculum, you encourage the child to feel glad he is there and to want to be part of what is going on. This, in turn, provides impetus to adopt the classroom ethos and follow it.

It is important to recognize that there is a difference between built-in opportunities for joy and enthusiasm and for rewards. A reward is conditional on one's doing something first. A "built-in opportunity for joy and enthusiasm" is unconditional. It happens simply because one is in the right place at the right time. Think of it as being unconditional in the way math is unconditional. Whatever your behavior, math still happens at ten o'clock.

There is an unfortunate tendency to believe that because opportunities for joy and enthusiasm are fun, they are thus good targets for being withdrawn in response to bad behavior or given out in response to good behavior. Again, this is making it conditional. This makes it a reward and not built in. While it is all well and good to reward especially positive behavior with a nice activity, there should also be some genuinely unconditional nice activities in the curriculum where children can feel enthusiasm for being in the class and experience joy, even though they have had a really crappy day.

You may need to be quite structured initially when providing these opportunities in the classroom. Most such activities have a certain amount of chaos inherent in them, and until children are used to dealing with happy emotions without losing the plot entirely, lack of structure may be a real problem.

Similarly, you may encounter some children who have no idea how to behave in an unstructured situation. This doesn't mean these children should never have unstructured activities. It means you will need to actively teach appropriate behavior and be tolerant while they are learning it.

Torey used cooking, art, music, and movement as her main sources of joyful activity and fostered enthusiasm by talking about the activities ahead of time. She asked the child to picture what was going to happen or what he wanted to do in the activity and made enthusiastic comments such as "Won't that be fun?" or "I'm looking forward to that."

Spontaneity helps enthusiasm develop. Learn to recognize potential "Hey, let's have fun" moments when you suddenly throw over routine and *play*. Snowstorms are particularly wonderful for this, not only for the obvious delight of playing in the snow but also for the occasion of doing something different when only a few students turn up for class and you can afford to play. Other times, however, also work well, including occasionally when everyone is teetering on the brink of implosion. A sudden change to a lighthearted or humorous activity can divert rage into enthusiasm, especially if coupled with a complete change of activity level from quiet to dramatically active or active to dramatically quiet. Some examples of this include the following:

- Songs. Stop what you are doing for a musical interlude, including instruments, if they are handy.
- Dancing or actions. Again, just spontaneously interrupt the work for free-form dancing, jumping jacks, running in place, and so on.
- Silly voices or exaggerated facial expressions.

Again, it's important to remember that you may need to have *structured* spontaneity to start with, as some children may not initially be able to cope with the chaos of ordinary spontaneity without going off the deep end. This doesn't mean planning/aforethought, which doesn't really qualify as spontaneous. Rather it means monitoring the activity well so that the usual rules of the structured classroom routine are kept in place. For example, Torey often used a stretching activity during which she would choose one of the children to come up front, and she would pull her through the activities like a puppet while the other children followed along. It was part of their normal structure, so the children knew what she was doing and when she usually did it. However, sometimes when the children were particularly *antsy* or if someone was getting way too wound up in a situation, Torey would spontaneously do the stretching activity, grabbing the suspect kid and getting everyone else to drop what they were doing and follow along. The familiarity provided enough structure that chaotic kids didn't go wild and the spontaneity of the activity was surprising enough to change the mood.

BUILD IN OPPORTUNITIES FOR EXPRESSION OF FEELINGS

Much misbehavior revolves around inappropriately expressed feelings. It's important to accept that people have an entire range of strong feelings. Classroom management isn't about eliminating the expression of such feelings but about teaching the child to express them in a fitting manner. By building in occasions to express feelings, we move emotions from a control issue to a teaching opportunity wherein we can help the child learn how to direct his emotions appropriately.

The following are helpful ways to tackle difficult emotions and emotional behavior:

- *Name feelings.* Much misbehavior stems from emotion outstripping an individual's ability to express what is happening to him or her. Learning to articulate feelings tends to have a dramatic effect of the ability to control them because then what has previously needed to be expressed physically can be expressed verbally. Many children have not made the connection between what they are feeling and how they are acting, which makes it very difficult for them to get control of the emotion.

So verbalize emotions whenever possible to help establish this connection between feelings and behavior. "You're feeling angry. It makes you want to hit Jesse." "You're feeling excited. You want to bounce about."

- *Teach children how to identify feelings in others.* Many children have real difficulty reading other people's facial expressions and body language. This is especially true of children on the autistic spectrum, but it is generally true for most children in special classes. Actively teach expression recognition using still photographs from magazines, and other sources. Also use video, where you can freeze the frame and ask the children to say what comes next based on the character's body language and facial features. Make them "feelings detectives."

- *Make it acceptable to acknowledge the complete range of emotions.* We all have them. We all have all of them. Some feelings are vile and socially unacceptable, but that doesn't stop them from being there. Acknowledging feelings verbally validates the child's ability to judge what is happening inside herself and is often sufficient to help her keep control of them.

- *Make it acceptable to express feelings, but keep control of the ways in which they are expressed.* "You're feeling angry. But I can't allow you to hurt David. You can use words or you can draw me a picture of how angry you feel."

- *Actively teach appropriate ways of expressing feelings.* There are numerous acceptable ways to put across even very difficult emotions. The ultimate goal is verbal—being able to identify, express, and defuse emotions with words—because this is the mature, human way of handling feelings without suppressing or repressing them. The arts are an excellent intermediary here, allowing a child to express the intensity of the emotion, and then latterly learn to articulate it. Painting, drawing, writing, dancing, and making music all work well. You can also use abstract physical exercise such as running, working out, and even screaming in acceptable places. We are less convinced about the value of punching bags and other concrete physical expressions for dealing with anger, however, as our experience has been that this seems to prolong or increase aggressive tendencies.

In addition to catching emotions when they happen and diverting them into teaching opportunities, it is helpful to build opportunities into the classroom structure to acknowledge, discuss, express, and troubleshoot emotions. This gives children the chance to explore this critical area when in a calm state when they can think more clearly and retain more easily.

Ways of building opportunities to deal with emotion into the daily routine include the following:

- *Opening and closing circle.* Torey always had a circle to start the day and finish the day where the children gathered around either in chairs or on the floor. Opening exercises included greeting everyone, show-and-tell activities, and her discussing a general outline of the day. Closing exercises included assessment of how things had gone, positive feedback, and good-byes. It was during these circles that Torey often brought up social issues the group was having and had an open discussion of how to resolve them or alternately posed questions about how to deal with certain issues.

- *Court.* If Torey had a persistent social problem that involved several children but couldn't be solved in a circle, they occasionally held a court where one side had the floor and explained his or her perspective, and then the other side had his or her say. Torey used a baton to represent a courtroom gavel, and whoever had the baton could speak, but no one else could in order to keep interruptions to a minimum. Once both sides had given their views, they discussed the matter as a whole group and came up with a judgment.

- *Drama and role-playing.* Role-playing is an extremely useful tool for teaching all sorts of things, and most children once they are used to it enjoy it enormously. Using role-play, one can exaggerate emotions to make them clearer and then practice different methods of dealing with them

- *Music.* If a pharmaceutical company had discovered music and made a pill of it, we would all be demanding a prescription. It's that effective. Yet it is often greatly neglected in the classroom. Making music is a wonderful way of expressing emotions appropriately, but equally important is listening to music. Recognize music's way of affecting emotions, of calming and soothing, of enlivening, and of lifting spirits. Five minutes of closed eyes, imagining what they heard in Beethoven's Pastoral symphony sorted out more classroom dramas for Torey than almost any other prescriptive method.

- *Language arts.* Often children can express on paper what they can't in face-to-face words. Torey's kids wrote every day, usually for about 20 minutes, even in the lowest classes. They all kept journals in which they could record anything they wanted, and she often used these to dialogue with the children (which means, of course, checking the journals every day and responding promptly to anything a child says in them.) As they became comfortable with the medium, she often used it to diffuse highly charged situations by sending combatants off to write down their side of the story (or illustrate it, if words failed). This often gave the children much needed space and a chance to calm down without the punishment aspect of a time-out spell. They could focus their minds on what actually went wrong and how it made them feel.

BUILD IN OPPORTUNITIES TO COMMUNICATE WITH YOU

It should go without saying that a relationship-driven methodology means the focus is on relationships, but it is amazing how often we forget that communication is the engine that drives all significant relationships. To forge helpful, meaningful relationships with the children, you need to communicate well with them, but they also need to be able to communicate well with you. The easiest way to ensure this is to build communication opportunities into the regular classroom structure:

- *Ensure they know you* want *to communicate with them.* You do this foremost by paying attention. Notice their behavior, their personal changes, what interests them, and what they care about. And listen when they talk.
- *Kobold's Box or similar recognition activities.* In *One Child*, Torey's class had what was called the Kobold's Box. The kobold was supposed to be a little invisible fairy who kept an eye out for good behavior, good deeds, and so forth, and he supposedly slipped little notes into the Kobold's Box about what he'd seen. At closing circle each day, Torey would open the box and read the notes. Obviously most of the notes she put in herself, but the children were also encouraged to *help* the kobold and write notes.
- *Suggestion box.* Similar to the Kobold's Box is a suggestion box where people can leave notes, either anonymous or signed, and suggestions about things that need to be talked about or dealt with. For example, one child used the suggestion box to disclose that his family had no food in the house and it had been almost 48 hours since his previous meal. Another child disclosed persistent bullying was happening on the playground, which gave the group a chance to sort it out.
- *Opening and closing circle.* The primary focus of circle is communication, and once children are used to the format, the predictability of its happening twice a day increases participation. To encourage children to use it as an opportunity to communicate with her, Torey tried to include discussions of their pastimes, out-of-school activities, television programs, plans, and so on, as well as troubleshooting classroom problems. She always came with a *poser*, a question of which to ask their opinions, in case conversation flagged.

BUILD IN OPPORTUNITIES TO TEACH STRESS-REDUCTION AND RELAXATION SKILLS

When confronted with stress, the majority of children with behavioral disorders are unable to successfully calm themselves down. They are also unable to recognize ways to structure self-healing. Methods they may have alighted on to cope with these problems are often inappropriate or chaotic, such as head banging, aggression, drug or alcohol abuse, or inappropriate eating.

We need to recognize that the world we live in is stressful. The media is constantly priming us for threats of terrorism, violent crime, pandemic diseases, economic disaster, and environmental catastrophe on top of the personal problems we all experience with families, relationships, work/school, and health. Our hurried, future-oriented society provides few opportunities for natural relaxation. With a focus on accomplishing goals, children are often not given the opportunity to waste time doing nothing, to spend time away from media, or to engage in activities that don't have a clear outcome. Because their activities and their behavior are generally controlled externally by others, who arrange the schedules and provide the payoffs, many children turn naturally to external means of stress control as well. Means such as television and computer games, and on the more serious end, drugs and alcohol, don't allow children to develop an internal ability to soothe themselves. In our experience, children profit markedly from being taught relaxation skills in a direct manner as part of the ordinary curriculum. It is helpful to incorporate these activities from the onset when creating a classroom:

- *Structure your day so that high-impact activities are interspersed with low-impact activities.* This is an obvious one, and most of us no doubt already endeavor to do this with our classes. However, explain this aloud. Show what you are doing so that children can perceive the pattern and learn to structure themselves this way.

- *Call attention to the need to relax.* Many children do not recognize when they are reaching the tipping point, none more so than children with attention and impulse disorders. It is important to label stress so that children can learn to identify it and then help them link that feeling to the need to engage in relaxing activities.

Useful forms of relaxation or stress-lowering activities for the classroom include the following:

- *Exercise.* Sending the children off on a run around the playground, having them perform jumping jacks in class, or doing anything aerobic that makes everyone puff are all usually very helpful in reducing stress. Sunlight also helps. Ten minutes of fast-paced activity outside on a sunny day can do wonders.
- *Spontaneous movement.* This can be creative dance movements to music or even less formal than that. If there is a long period of sitting, often call a break and do what is referred to as *puppeting.* Choose a child to be your puppet and pull him through the movements of head, shoulders, knees, and toes while the other children copy.
- *Laughter and humor.* Never miss a chance to laugh. Absolutely *nothing* is as relaxing and de-stressing as laughter. Help children see the funny side in things and indulge in giggling with them. Include activities that will raise a laugh.
- *Relaxation exercises: meditation and deep breathing.* These are the traditional relaxation exercises, and it is extremely helpful to become familiar with them. They can be an absolute godsend in the classroom when everyone is getting on one another's nerves and irritability is rampant. Meditation is the best known of these. Most younger children, even the wild ones, are natural meditators and will enthusiastically take part in meditation, if it is kept very short but happens often. All that is required for meditation is to have the children sit up straight in

a chair or on the floor and to provide an explanation to them that meditation is resting your mind. Resting your mind when it gets tired is just like resting your body when it gets tired.

o The classic way to do meditation is to close eyes and gently follow the breath in and out—through the nose, with the rising and falling of the chest or the abdomen. It doesn't matter which. Alternately, they can close their eyes and focus on a sound in the classroom, like the heating system or birds outside.

o Explain to the children that it is normal to have thoughts pop into their heads while they are doing this, but as their minds are resting now, their minds don't want to bother with thoughts or feelings right now. They can think about the thoughts later. Tell them, "For now just let the thoughts go and bring your attention back to your breath." Liken the thoughts to butterflies or clouds—anything that can float off—and describe how we want to just let them go and not chase after them.

o One or two minutes at a time is enough. It is better to do it short and often rather than long and boring.

Meditation is an extremely useful skill for children to learn, and most will really get into it if done regularly (and will pester you for it, if you forget!). The ones who find it hardest are usually the ones who need it most, so it is worth persisting.

Deep-breathing exercises are another good type of relaxation. These normally come from yoga, and again, most children really enjoy the slow, physical posing that is a natural part of yoga. But you can also just use the breathing exercises. Many of these are available on CDs that can be used in the classroom.

● *Music.* As mentioned previously, music is your friend. Invite it in often. Classical music, ambient music, and music specially designed for slowing brain waves are all widely available and often very reasonable. And these make excellent relaxation tools. Consider playing this kind of music occasionally when the children are working, partly because it is effective then too in helping them focus but also partly to get them used to the sound, as many will not have been exposed to this kind of music before. For relaxation purposes, play it at times when the children can focus on it and not simply have it as background noise. *Listening* to the music gives them the space to calm down.

- *Your reading aloud.* Most children enjoy being read to and this tends to be an excellent way to slow the day down and give children a chance to relax and calm down.
- *Guided visualization.* This, like music, is another highly effective classroom tool that is easily available, very cheap to use, and incredibly versatile. It has the added benefit that most children enjoy it enormously. There are many examples of good guided visualizations available on CD or in books, but in our experience, the best are the ones made up in the moment, which keeps them ever fresh and always pertinent to your particular group. You don't need to be a master storyteller to do this. There doesn't need to be any plot in what you are telling; just give description to allow children to engage as many senses as possible through their imagination. If you need stimulation, use pictures from magazines like *National Geographic* to provide inspiration for a trip under the sea, to the mountains, or the like. Have the children assume a relaxed posture, and simply talk them through what you are looking at, using a soft, calming voice and as much open-ended, multisensory detail as you can manage. Even very hyper children or those with mild autism can usually be drawn into guided visualization if it is detailed enough that they do not have to rely overmuch on their own imagination.

Guided visualization works well as a relaxation exercise, as a means of calming a group down, or reorienting them. It is also a successful way of giving the children a break when they can't go outside. On these occasions, use a livelier scene, such as a safari or a circus, or an imagined activity, such as flying.

6

Relationship Skills

For a relationship-driven classroom to work, significant relationships need to form between student and teacher and among the students themselves. Many children coming into special education classes will have inadequate or inappropriate relationship skills, due to dysfunctional current or former environments, lack of experience, poor social skills, neurological differences such as autism, or a combination of these. The ability to form strong, healthy bonds with others is crucial to the successful functioning of a relationship-driven methodology. And as the lack of these bonds will contribute significantly not only to emotional and behavioral issues in the classroom but also to everything in the child's life, it is best to directly and actively teach the most crucial relationship skills right from the beginning of the school year.

All children are capable of forming meaningful relationships. Some, such as those on the autistic spectrum or with attachment disorders, will find some aspects of relationship building challenging, but this does not mean they are unable to form relationships, and it certainly doesn't mean the children don't want to. Indeed, their challenges simply highlight the advantages of directly teaching relationship skills right from the beginning.

It is worth noting that while we strongly advocate direct and active teaching of various social and personal skills, we think it is better to integrate the teaching of these skills into the general curriculum whenever possible. Social and personal skills integrate well with ordinary subjects and with common classroom practices to the point that it is less a matter of making time to teach yet another subject than it is to modify what is already in place in order to strengthen relationships in the process.

We have divided the skills into those which are generally perceived as social or emotional intelligence skills and those which are more practical skills. By social or emotional intelligence, we don't mean social skills per se, although obviously the better a child's social skills, the more adept he is going to be at relationships. Rather, we are referring to those aspects of personal, social, and emotional development that are integral to a relationship-focused milieu. Most of these are skills which society often expects children to learn intuitively but that children with emotional or behavioral disorders need direct and active help in developing to a useful level.

ACTIVELY TEACH SEEING THINGS FROM ANOTHER PERSPECTIVE

Seeing things from another perspective involves developing a degree of objectivity. Objectivity simply means the ability to recognize that others may experience things differently than we do, and this results in different motivations or different reactions to ours. At its most developed stage, objectivity allows us to project ourselves into the perspective of others and to see how the world looks from their point of view. The inability to do this, to put oneself in another person's shoes, is, in our experience, the single greatest impediment to good social skills, and, oftentimes also to good behavior. When we can perceive how another person is interpreting a situation or see ourselves as others see us, this makes it much easier for us to regulate our behavior accordingly.

It is important to mention that the ability to see things from another perspective is *not* the same as empathy. Empathy is the subjective experience of feeling others' feelings as if what happened to them had happened to us—that crinkle in the stomach, for example, when someone tells us about being hit in the stomach themselves or the tears we shed upon hearing someone else's bad news. Seeing from another point of view means trying to go out of ourselves and our own perspective in an effort to understand what it is like to be the other person. Empathy, in contrast, is bringing the other person's circumstances into ourselves and experiencing them as if they were our own. Empathy has an important role to play in relationships, but it is not the skill we are talking about here.

The ability to see things from another perspective normally starts to arise developmentally about 15 to 18 months of age. Functional parents will recognize a child's efforts to see how the world is affecting others and reinforce it, saying things such as "Thank you for bringing me a tissue. You saw I needed one, didn't you?" or actively teaching it by saying things such as "How do you think your brother feels when you hit him?" or "Poor kitty. Look. You can tell he doesn't like getting squirted with the hose." However, children in dysfunctional families or children who spend much of their waking time in passive or individual pursuits, such as watching television or videos, or in large groups with a low adult-to-child ratio, such as in poorly staffed day care centers, will often miss out on this crucial feedback. As a consequence, the concept of stopping one's own thoughts and feelings in order to move out of one's own point of view and into another person's perspective to see how he thinks and feels about something can remain foreign territory.

Some of the ways of directly teaching this skill include the following:

- *Teach actively with materials,* as if it were a standard subject.
- *Make flashcards* with pictures from magazines that show different facial expressions. Play recognition games with them, use them as flash cards, and otherwise make certain

children can easily discern what facial expressions mean. Have children scour old magazines to make collages of their own feelings or of a given feeling, and so forth.

- *Teach children where to look to decode expressions.* Many children with social deficits will concentrate on the wrong facial parts, like mouths, or they do not look at the person at all. Help them understand the importance of looking at eyes and at facial expressions, and remind them to do this in the classroom, if necessary.
- *Freeze video/DVD frames* and have the children guess what comes next from the expressions or actions of the people.
- *Read stories and then have the children retell a story from the perspective of a different character.* This works especially well with very familiar stories like fairy tales. Have them rewrite the story of the "Three Bears" from the bears' perspective or "Red Riding Hood" from the wolf's perspective.
- *Use role-play.* Have children act out different emotions or create a game of charades where a child draws a card, expresses the emotion, and the others have to guess what it is.

ACTIVELY TEACH BODY LANGUAGE

As alluded to previously about seeing from another perspective, we get a huge amount of our social information from facial expressions and body language. Many children in classes for behavioral disorders have difficulty reading this intuitive language, so it is helpful to teach these skills actively. Start by teaching children to always look first at the eyes, then the rest of the face, and then to look for nonverbal clues in the body. In our experience, a fun introduction to this is with animals and pictures of animals. Many children respond much more freely when trying to read an animal's emotions than a human's. To teach the recognition of human emotions, use pictures from magazines or freeze frames of video material. Often children enjoy freezing frames of recordings of themselves and analyzing the expressions and body language.

Demonstrate how to apply this knowledge. Continually encourage and reinforce this skill by asking or saying such things as "How is he feeling?" "What's that feel like to her?" "What do you think he's thinking about?" or "How can you tell?"

When conflict arises, show the children how to apply expressions and body language to understand the other person's perspective. This will be very hard for children initially because they are so caught up in their emotions, and most body language is fleeting. Always ask at some point, "How do you think she saw it?" Always insist the child give his version of the *other* child's perspective. Then talk about how you can tell this by looking at facial expressions and body language for clues. It is helpful occasionally to have the child act out the other child's part, as in "How did Sandy feel when you broke the toy? What expression was on Sandy's face?"

Children with certain disabilities or differences will need extra support. Those on the autistic spectrum, in particular, find nonsubjective thinking very difficult. It is almost impossible for these children to project themselves accurately into another point of view without extensive help. Most are capable of enormous sensitivity and thoughtfulness and do genuinely want to master this skill. But they will often require careful teaching, sometimes starting at a very basic level, and real sensitivity on the teacher's part to keep them from feeling discouraged. It is helpful, as a teacher, to be prepared for this and to be more flexible with these students.

ACTIVELY TEACH SELF-AWARENESS

Self-awareness is the ability to be conscious of ourselves. Important aspects of self-awareness include

- cognitive awareness of what we feel and think;
- cognitive awareness of the difference between us and our actions;
- cognitive awareness of the capacity to make choices about ourselves;

- an understanding that what we experience is unique to us as an individual and others may not experience the same thing in the same way (an understanding of subjectivity);
- learning how to *pull back* and look at ourselves and what we are feeling, thinking, and doing;
- becoming aware of our thinking as we're doing it;
- learning to see our actions as they look to others (an understanding of objectivity);
- becoming aware of our self-image;
- understanding the differences between our self-image, the way others see us, and how we really are; and
- understanding how to close the gap between who we are and how others perceive us or alternately, understanding why we choose to maintain it.

Many of these are very high-level skills that people seldom master until adolescence or even adulthood, but most self-awareness skills will start to make their first appearances in fits and starts during middle childhood. Directly introducing and teaching these skills helps the child understand how to identify them and that they are valuable.

How to directly teach self-awareness can be accomplished using methods such as the following:

1. *Language arts.* Writing provides an excellent tool for teaching self-awareness. Many children are willing to explore awareness of their emotions and behavior on paper, and the slowness of writing gives them time to think. Journaling makes writing a regular habit, and the subject matter is generally determined by the student. But also assign topics for writing, such as "What do you like to do when you are alone?" or "If you could be an animal, what would you be?"

2. *Polls.* Torey's children loved polls where they got a chance to list likes, dislikes, and patterns of behavior

(what do you do to get ready for bed?). She often put them up on the bulletin board, and children could answer at leisure and tack their answer up. Others enjoyed reading the answers and they often prompted discussion.

3. *Opening and closing circle.* In circle, tackle self-awareness directly by talking about things like self-image or seeing how things look differently from different perspectives and how we learned to assess that for ourselves. As long as the circle is well supervised so that bullying can't occur, it is a good opportunity for children to help each other with awareness. It is also a good setting for troubleshooting problem areas of awareness.

4. *Movement and rhythmic activities.* Occasionally, doing slow, rhythmic yoga-type movements helps students relax and increases their ability to tell where their body is in space. It also helps break rapid-thinking situations where the child is reacting and unable to stop long enough to discern what he is doing.

5. *"Freeze."* This is just a game, but we have found it useful for all sorts of purposes. All that is involved is that anytime the teacher says, "Freeze," all the students must immediately stop what they are doing, freeze into whatever position they are in, and hold it until the teacher says, "Thaw." This is an excellent way to divert chaos or to quickly slow things down if you see calamity coming, but it is also a helpful self-awareness activity if followed up very briefly by asking each student to say what she was thinking, feeling, or doing at that moment. To be effective, "Freeze" shouldn't be used as a disciplinary tool and should be done with good humor so that it does not develop negative associations. Most children appreciate the minibreak it provides and enjoy telling the teacher about what they were doing at that exact moment.

ACTIVELY TEACH COMMONALITY

Commonality simply means what we have in common. Please be aware that a duality exists in the relationship-driven approach, and it is important to teach both halves when trying to strengthen relationship skills. One half is awareness of our tendency to be very subjective. A lot of our relationship problems come about because we think only from our point of view. We don't see the bigger picture, and we don't appreciate that others see things differently but just as legitimately. So, as teachers we must actively teach that the rest of the world doesn't think just like you and that if you want to avoid problems and enjoy happiness, you need to let go of the notion that your thinking is the only kind. *But*—and this is very important—the flip side of this is that in fact we are all alike. We are all much *more* alike than different.

This is sophisticated, this idea that we need to keep in mind that we are all different but at the same time all alike. But kids generally get their heads around it straightforwardly if it is pointed out to them. This same duality of specific versus general occurs in many, many other common forms, so we all have plenty of experience of it. Use the word *levels* to make it more understandable, saying that on one level we all think differently, and so we must remember not to fall into the trap of thinking everyone else sees things just the way we do. But on another bigger, more important level, we are all alike, because we are all people. Everyone else in the world, for example, experiences the same kinds of feelings we do. Everyone knows what feeling sad or scared or happy is like. And everyone's bodies also experience the same kinds of things, such as getting hurt or falling ill.

It is important to teach this concept of commonality—of everyone being basically alike—as part of self-awareness to help children integrate the idea that while certain of our thoughts and feelings are unique to us, we are all much more alike than different. This allows us to feel connected to others.

Reasons for teaching commonality are to dissuade old thinking patterns that lead to feelings of disconnection because

- lack of understanding of commonality creates us-and-them thinking. This inhibits the formation of a single cohesive social unit in the classroom.
- lack of understanding of commonality inhibits a sense of belonging and, thus, by default, a sense of inclusion.
- lack of understanding of commonality is frequently at the root of bullying. Teaching commonality and actively practicing it normally decreases bullying markedly in the classroom.
- lack of understanding of commonality is one of the major underpinnings of prejudice and intolerant behavior. It contributes directly to racism, bigotry, religious fanaticism, hate crimes, and similar problems.
- lack of understanding of commonality also tends to contribute directly to dangerous or ineffective self-concepts children may have about themselves, such as that they are no good, evil, worthless, crazy, or alone. This feeds the child's belief that he or she is incapable of becoming a good or competent person.
- lack of understanding of commonality can cause us to be judgmental of other people. Learning commonality lets us realize that the other person, *however* different, bad, repugnant, or difficult, is really just like us under the skin. Commonality helps us understand he or she is not a beast or inhuman but simply doesn't know how to be different at this time and place.

Teaching commonality is an ongoing process. It isn't something you teach in a unit and say, "Okay, this is done; you've got it." You are doing it all the time because it is something people forget. There are three main methods that are useful to directly teach commonality.

1. *Point out commonality* a lot. The easiest way to teach it is simply to talk about it frequently, pointing it out in everyday situations in order to raise awareness of it. Reinforce children for noticing it themselves by means such as the following:

   o Use magazine pictures that show very different types of people (people who dress very differently, are of different age groups, gender, cultures, and so on) to the children in the class. Then ask the children to predict all the things that person will do when she gets up in the morning, when she is tired, and so forth. Help children understand that everyone, no matter how different on the outside, will need to eat, to sleep, to eliminate, to spend time with loved ones, and will want to do something interesting. Everyone will experience such things as pleasure at getting something new, fear of losing loved ones, illness, disappointment, pride, and more.

   o Use popular press stories of celebrities and sports stars to explore commonalities. Most kids love the idea of seeing inside such people and finding out they are just like them.

   o Have them identify normal emotions or emotional reactions in people who are different from themselves, and then actively connect these emotions to the children's own feelings.

2. *Teach that all people have both good and bad in them, and that this is normal, that this is how we are made.* Our task as competent human beings is to choose how we live. Sometimes we make wrong choices, so the next time we choose, it is important to choose differently. Actively teach how *everyone* is this way, that this is one of our commonalities, and so a bad person isn't really different than us. He has just chosen wrongly. Make it clear that everyone struggles when trying to change themselves from doing something they shouldn't to something they should. Personal change is a difficult activity for everyone. Understanding this makes the

child more tolerant of others struggling to change, but also tends to make him more hopeful about changing himself. It helps shift thinking from "I'm a failure. There's something wrong with me" to "I failed this time, but everyone struggles with personal changes, and we just have to keep trying."

3. *Teach that it is normal to be afraid of things we don't know but that we are able to choose a different way to act.* Show how fear of the unknown is, in fact, a point of commonality, and everyone feels like this to some degree in new situations. If something makes us afraid, we often don't think clearly and react instead of act. Talk about how other people, even very different people (different races, difference cultures, different genders, different ages, different religious groups, and so forth) in this situation will be feeling the same way. Discuss, brainstorm, or role-play ways of dealing with this typical fear, including acknowledging that the other person may be feeling the same.

ACTIVELY TEACH THE DIFFERENCE BETWEEN A PERSON AND A PERSON'S ACTIONS

In order to relate in a warm and tolerant manner, we must accept that each person is ultimately separate from his or her actions and thus has the potential to control and change his or her behavior.

What *is* the person? For our purposes, the person who we are) is simply the sum of all our parts—our body, our mind, our thoughts, our feelings, and our actions but also our personal history, our family history, our cultural history, our genetic makeup, and so forth. As discussed in an earlier chapter, rather the way the United States refers to all the separate states put together and acting as a whole, *I* refers to all parts of us put together and acting as a whole. Actions are just one part of this whole and not the whole itself. Actions are what we do and not who we are.

It is crucial to understand this distinction between what we do and who we are. We cannot change who we are. We *can* change what we do. Actions belong to us, and in that way they are part of us and we are responsible for them, but they are only one part of a greater whole. They are not the whole itself. This is one of the most basic tenants of the relationship-driven approach. It is this concept that powers the confidence that change *can* take place, no matter how appalling the current circumstances. Self-esteem can be rebuilt, motivation can be reinstilled, and new lives can take form as long as there is the hope that this is possible. And this hope resides in the understanding that what we do is not who we are.

As teachers, it is imperative we actively maintain this optimism regarding the possibility of change. There is not much point in being in the classroom if we don't genuinely believe people can change. Likewise, it is important to instill this hopefulness in the children.

The following are some successful ways to directly teach that actions are different from who we are:

1. *Actions are our public face.* People can't see inside our heads, so they don't know our precise thoughts. Consequently, they judge us on our actions. Role-playing and discussions of where thoughts and actions differ help illustrate this. For example, use a story about a boy stealing a pumpkin from outside a store. In one instance, he steals it because he wants a Halloween pumpkin and doesn't want to pay for it. In another instance, he steals it just to throw it in the road and smash it. In a third instance, he steals it because he wants to make a jack-o'-lantern for his young, disabled sister at home but can't afford to buy one. In a fourth version, he steals it because his mother gave him money to buy it, but bullies stole the money from him, and his mother will get very angry with him if he returns without the pumpkin. His thoughts and motives were very different in the four versions, but others can only see his actions.

2. *Actions can be changed.* We can't change into what circumstances we are born, who our parents are, what our ethnicity is, what our society is like, and what genes we were given. These are all parts of who we are as a person. Actions, however, are different. They are what we are, and we can choose to change those. Using the same story, get the children to brainstorm different ways the boy could act in those scenarios where his circumstances can't change. For example, how could he act differently and still get a pumpkin for his disabled sister? Or how else could he handle the bullies who took his money?

3. *Actions are changed by becoming aware of our thoughts and feelings before we act, then choosing to do something different.* The way to change behavior is to become aware we are about to do something before we actually have done it and then actively choosing to do something different. This is hard. Personal change is hard. There is an instinctive push to do things as we are used to doing them. This is the animal part of our brain reassuring us we are safe with familiar things, even when in reality the familiar things are getting us into deep trouble, whether it be through repeatedly eating the wrong kinds of food and becoming overweight or through repeatedly smacking people on the nose when they annoy us. Nonetheless, not only is this is how change happens; it's also the only way change happens.

Some actions have become automatic, so it doesn't feel like we are thinking before we do them. It feels like they are just happening, but the truth is, we are thinking first. It may be in a very fast *autopilot* sort of way, and so it can take practice to catch these thoughts when they happen, but this is how change is actually done: First awareness, and then choosing a different action.

Because many children (and adults!) do not initially believe that there are thoughts in front of many impulsive actions, particularly ones involving emotions, it's easy to show students that this is true. Use the following illustration: If someone suddenly pulled a banana out of his pocket and pointed it at you, you would look at it and feel surprised. Probably you would start to laugh or giggle. This happens very fast, so that you might start to laugh almost immediately on seeing the banana, but you are laughing because your thoughts tell you that a banana is harmless, and thus, he is being a bit silly doing that. However, if he suddenly pulled a gun out of his pocket and pointed it at you, your reaction would be just as fast. You would get frightened, and you might jump out of your seat. You might even run or try to hide. The sense of fear would be almost immediate. Nonetheless, it is happening because your thoughts have told you the gun is dangerous. If a little baby were sitting in the classroom along with us, he wouldn't feel afraid when I pulled the gun out because he hasn't learned yet that the gun is dangerous, so his thoughts would not tell him to be afraid. He would just sit there, looking at it. Now, for a third scenario: The lighting in the room is a bit dim. The man pulls out a gun from his pocket and points it at you. Again, you would get frightened when you first saw it and might jump out of your seat or try to run away. This time, however, the gun is a fake. It is just a toy gun. Why did you jump? This is because your first thoughts are that guns are dangerous, and because you are thinking that, you react with fear, even though the gun isn't dangerous at all. When you could easily tell what he was thinking, you weren't afraid. When what he was holding was dangerous, you were immediately afraid. But when he was holding something that wasn't dangerous, you were also afraid. But once you know the gun is a fake (your changed thoughts), if he pulled it out again, you would not feel afraid (your changed action). This is an illustration of how thoughts always precede actions, even very strong emotional reactions that happen in a split second. But they also show how, once we become aware of something, we can change the action.

You Are Not Your Actions

You are a whole that is greater than the sum of its parts. Help children understand actions are only one part of who they are. Have them make up a list or a collage of all the things that make them *them*. Help them see that not only is it the things within themselves such as their likes and dislikes, their thoughts and feelings, and their body, but it is also their family history, where they were born, their ethnicity, the culture they were born into, the era in which they were born, and so much more that are all part of who they are.

Some Things Can Be Changed, Some Can't

In discussing who we are, help children recognize that some things about us can't ever be changed, so it is important not to focus on these things as the root of our problems. A good example of this is birth date. Most children can appreciate that this is something they cannot change, and they can understand how silly it would be to blame, say, not getting up on time for school on the date they were born. Explain how some of things we cannot change about ourselves are fortunate. For example, we were born in our country and not somewhere where people are repressed or punished for wanting basic freedoms. Some things about us that can't be changed are neutral and don't matter very much, like on which day of the week we were born. And all of us also have a few unfortunate things about us that can't be changed. For example, we might have skin that sunburns very easily. Some very thought-provoking discussions can happen over this topic, and it is often helpful to let children explore the less fortunate things that have happened to them, such as the families they were born into, the disabilities with which they have to cope, and such. It is important to help them understand that this is a universal experience. Everybody has some fortunate things, some unfortunate things, and some neutral things. Focus on helping the students differentiate between things that we can change (like our attitude and our actions) and things we can't (like where and when we were born). And acknowledge that there are gray areas (e.g., those things that we can't change right now), such as the socioeconomic level we were born into or the genetic condition we inherited, but which we may be able to change in the future, either because of our own actions, such as getting a good job that allows us to live more comfortably than our parents do, or because of collective actions, such as a medical breakthrough to help a genetic condition.

Sometimes All That Can Be Changed Is Our Attitude

In coming to understand the universality of circumstances that can't be changed, it is important to talk about how, even though we may be stuck in a very unfortunate situation that we can't change, we can still choose to think differently about it, and this is a type of action. This is a good place to introduce stories of inspirational people like Helen Keller.

Good and Bad People Versus Good and Bad Actions

It is very helpful to have frequent discussions about the concepts of good/right and bad/wrong, as this is one of the easiest ways to teach children how to distinguish between the person and the action. Ask, "When you say someone is bad/stupid/hopeless/and so on, what are you talking about?" Inevitably it comes down to something that has been done or not done—an action. Point out that the action *was* wrong but that this is only part of the person. Do a quick brainstorm of commonalities to show how much of the person himself isn't bad. This can often be done in a very humorous way, such as "So, he called you a name. Calling names is wrong, so his action was wrong. But was his stomach bad to you? His hair? His left elbow? His knee caps? His action was wrong, but look how much more there is to Johnny that didn't hurt you."

It Is Unhelpful to Be Intolerant or Judgmental About Things Over Which People Have No Control

It's very helpful to teach the concept that if something can't be changed presently, there's not much point getting upset about it. Most children learn this concept most easily with animals. Start with really obvious things, such as pointing out that a rabbit, for example, cannot open the door to its cage and come over to eat the carrot you are holding, no matter how much you might want it to. The rabbit is simply incapable of opening the lock on the cage door. Ever. So there is no point thinking it is a stupid rabbit if you are sitting across the room with a carrot in your hand. It isn't being stupid. It's doing the best it can, and we need to accept it for where it is at in its reasoning abilities. Most children can see this easily. Move on to more complex, grayer areas, such as how the rabbit scratches and struggles to get away when someone picks it up and holds it incorrectly. It doesn't know our thoughts and isn't able to think like a human, so it can't understand why it is being held that way and becomes frightened. Brainstorm with the children about what the rabbit might actually be thinking is happening. Help them understand that it's possible for the rabbit to learn not to be afraid and that would be nice, but we must teach it with our gentle behavior. In the meantime, the rabbit doesn't know that, so it can't change how it behaves. There is no point in thinking of it as a bad rabbit for scratching, because at this point, it can't help it. Convey to the children that it works better to think, "That's the way rabbits are, and it will take some time for the rabbit to learn how to be different."

The Parts of You That You Can Control Are Thoughts and Actions, so We Work With These to Make Changes

Again, and again, and again, reorient attention back to the fact that we focus only on the things we can change, and those are our thoughts and actions. The rest will follow of its own accord. For example, while we can't make ourselves not be ill when we are ill, if we change our actions such as eating healthily and exercising, our body will tend to follow this change and be ill less often. Or we could find our weak immune system is genetic and a part of us which is not able to be changed at this time, in which case, we would accept that.

You Are Valuable Just for Being Who You Are

Everybody matters. This is the bottom line.

ACTIVELY TEACH THAT EVERYONE *CAN* CHANGE

Occasionally people complain that maintaining the belief that everyone can change is a view of the world that is too idealistic or unrealistic. Nonsense. Being too idealistic would be saying that everyone *does* change. Being unrealistic would be *expecting* everyone to change. What we are maintaining is that everyone has the *potential* to change. We're not omniscient. We don't know all the factors. We can't see the future. All we've got is this tiny slice of the present, so we're not in a good position to be more judgmental than that. More to the point, if we, ourselves, genuinely don't believe in the potential to change for everyone, we don't belong in the classroom. It's just not fair to the kids.

Change can be slow, subtle, and difficult and very often happens in a manner much different to what we had planned or envisioned, so it is important children be aware of this and be aware that this is normal. We want to help children shift away from the goal oriented, judgmental perspective that says, "I tried. I failed. I can't do it. I give up," to the process-oriented perspective that says, "I tried. It didn't happen this time. I'll try again."

It is important to actively teach that everyone can change. It's kind of a step above optimism, perhaps more foundational than optimism, but it's just a basic belief in everyone's ability to change. Successful ways of teaching about change include the following concepts:

- *Change is hard.* This is perhaps the most important message to get across, because it is easy to become discouraged and give up when we fail. Help children understand personal change seldom happens overnight, and there are always slips and backslides, but this does not mean change isn't happening.

- *Failure is a normal part of change.* Failure is one of the most potent learning tools there is, so it is important to develop a realistic, reasonably positive attitude toward it rather than a doom-laden, end-of-the-world attitude. Learn to commiserate with the child rather than punish her for failing. This ensures you are on the same team, you and the child against the behavior, rather than you against the child and the behavior. The failure itself will usually be a natural consequence enough for the child in most instances without the added disappointment from the teacher. Help the child learn to respond to failure by seeing it as an approximation of the desired change or, if that is not possible, with a positive attitude toward the fact she tried. Approximations are a normal part of change. Normal learning means that there will be several approximations of the desired change before it happens completely. Help the child recognize approximations for the positive steps forward they are rather than shortfalls of the goal.

- *Backsliding is a normal part of change.* Everyone who makes a serious personal change will backslide at one point or another. Identify the backslide for what it is, and help the child recognize this is a temporary occurrence and not the loss of everything he worked for. Reassure him that he will get back on track quickly, and then teach the child how to troubleshoot to find out why it happened. Provide extra support and supervision, if necessary.

- *The secret to success is getting back on the horse.* It's very easy to interpret failure or backsliding as the end outcome and give up. Just as easy is to encounter a slip and think, "I might as well be hung for a sheep as a lamb" and respond by engaging in much more undesirable behavior. Most of us have our own personal experience of this in such areas as losing weight or trying to eat healthily, so it is important to understand children also will be thinking this way in response to failure.

There is one, and only one, way to succeed and that is to pick yourself up, dust yourself off, and get back on track immediately. No "I'll start anew tomorrow." Start anew *now*. Get back on the horse now. Torey taught this concept through the idea that failure isn't really failure unless you don't get back up. Slips and backslides are normal, and they are going to happen, but you haven't actually failed if you keep going. One of the most helpful ways of reinforcing this is to only record or acknowledge successful efforts at change. Don't ignore slips, however. This tends to encourage the child to believe either that she got away with it, and so it doesn't matter how the child herself responds, or else that you simply don't care how the child is doing. Instead, acknowledge slips matter-of-factly; then encourage the child to get back up with the reassurance that you understand how hard it is but that you know she will eventually succeed.

ACTIVELY TEACH WHAT GOES INTO POSITIVE ATTITUDES AND POSITIVE EMOTIONS

A positive attitude encourages strong relationships to form. It is also perhaps the single most important factor in making successful, personal changes. Many children in programs for the behaviorally disordered will not have a lot of experience of positive attitudes and emotions. Society in general does not regard exceptionalities as positive aspects, and negative behaviors tend to generate only negative responses. Very often people never look beyond the negative actions to the child behind it. As a consequence, children often arrive in special education feeling bad and negative and not fully aware there even are alternative perspectives possible. It is important, of course, to talk about emotions in general and to allow children to discuss and experience the commonality of negative emotions. It is crucial, however, to actively teach positive attitudes and emotions in order to encourage children to develop them. Among the positive emotions and attitudes that need to be taught are optimism, luck, and happiness.

Optimism

Optimism, as mentioned above, should already be a part of the teacher's emotional repertoire. It is important to also directly address optimism as a positive attitude that is worth encouraging in the classroom. Successful ways of doing this include the following:

- Label it when you see children demonstrating optimistic behavior in the classroom.
- Identify the feelings that go with optimism, such as "You're optimistic about the test today, aren't you? It feels good."
- Actively teach "looking on the bright side" by reorienting negative views. Don't go at this too vigorously, however, as there is a fine line between being positive and being annoyingly Pollyanna-ish. Torey had one child fall off the monkey bars during recess one day and break his arm. While she was in the nurse's office with him, waiting for his mother to come, he was moaning in pain. She leaned over and opened her mouth to say something but before she could, he interjected, "And now you're going to ask me to tell you something good about this," which was a clue to Torey that perhaps she was overdoing this!

Luck

Increasingly, research indicates that people who perceive themselves as lucky behave in ways that enhance the chances of their being lucky (Wiseman, 2003). Feeling lucky boosts our self-esteem and enhances our sense of the world being a positive place, so it is worth helping children facilitate luck.

Show that luck has to do with staying present. Torey often told the story of a little boy who was walking down a crowded street and found a coin. Then she talked with the class about why other people did not see the money—one man was busy thinking about his work, a woman was wondering whether she'd have enough money to buy a dress, a teenage boy was figuring out how to borrow the car from his dad, a teenage girl was thinking about her boyfriend, and so forth. Only the little boy was paying attention to where he was and what he was doing right then. Torey's students loved role-playing versions of this story.

Luck has been shown to stem largely from the ability to keep an eye out for good opportunities even while doing other things. One of Torey's favorite activities was to include a *luck* prize in schoolwork, folders, paperwork, or around the classroom. It was just a line or a picture or something similar midst all the normal things, and she would say, "You are lucky! If you come tell me you've seen this but don't tell anyone else, you'll get a reward." The rewards were always just minor things like stickers, and Torey did them randomly and seldom more often than once a week, but it greatly encouraged attentiveness and openness to lucky occurrences and made things more fun.

Research indicates that thinking you're lucky tends to make you lucky. Help the kids understand this concept, which is closely related to positive thinking, and help reinforce it with phrases such as "Isn't that lucky!" or "Aren't you lucky?" when good things happen that are not a direct result of the child's or someone else's actions to increase their attentiveness to good things.

Happiness

Obviously, we all want to be happy, and equally obvious, life is much easier to cope with when we are happy. However, in a predominantly goal-oriented culture, we often mistake happiness as a goal, as something to achieve rather than the ongoing process that it actually is. Because it is such an important part of quality-of-life and contributes so much to healthy relationships, it is helpful to directly teach about happiness.

Successful ways of doing this include the following:

- *Identify and label happiness when it is happening* such that children acquire a working knowledge of what it is and when it occurs. Many children are victims of advertising, stories, and television programs that equate happiness with the achievement of major goals. Make it clear that happiness is found frequently in the small, ordinary moments of every day.
- *Show how happiness is always in the process and not in the goal*, that it is something that can only be experienced "now," and that if we are focused on some future event, we can't actually feel what we're feeling now. One of the ways Torey taught this was to discuss what phrases like stop and smell the daisies meant. Most children do have an innate sense of this, if it is pointed out to them, but they need help in developing cognitive awareness. Our "Freeze" game was also a good way to assess if happiness was happening (and obviously more likely, if you call "Freeze" during a fun activity!). It was also helpful in bringing awareness to the concept that if we get too caught up in achieving a goal, we actually neglect to notice feeling happy.
- *Talk about the difference between pleasure and happiness.* In a predominantly goal-oriented world, instant gratification often gets confused with genuine happiness (e.g., because people believe happiness is a goal, they assume more quickly achieving the goal, instant gratification, will make them feel happy faster). Because happiness isn't in the goal but in the process, achieving the goal, however fast, often ends up feeling empty. Help children understand that the good feeling they have at the point they achieve something is pleasure. Pleasure is a sensation that we feel when something good happens, whether it is something we ourselves make happen or

whether something nice happens to us. Like all sensations, it doesn't last. This is why, when you achieve a goal, it feels good for a while, but then the feeling goes away and you have to achieve something else to experience it again. The opposite of pleasure is pain, and that's the sensation we experience when something bad happens. Happiness is different. It is a state of being rather than a sensation, so it can last, but it only happens in the present, as we are living it. Achieving goals can help us be happy, but this is the feeling we have over the longer term that comes from knowing we are capable. The strong initial feeling that occurs straight after achievement and then fades is pleasure.

- *Talk about contentment.* Contentment means being happy with what you *don't* have as well as what you do have. It is a kind of happiness and also a state of mind. It is another feeling we only experience in the process. It isn't possible to be content next week. We can only be content now. Children often need help understanding that it is possible to be working toward a goal but at the same time to feel happy with where you are right now, even though you haven't achieved it, because you know you are trying and you are working hard. This is contentment. If you feel that who you are right now isn't very good because you haven't achieved your goals yet, this will make you feel discontent. Show how sometimes discontentment is helpful because it spurs us on to make changes, but many times it is unhelpful because we feel so bad about ourselves that we find it hard to keep trying. Many children will have got into the habit of giving themselves lots of negative self-messages about not achieving. These kids often need active permission to feel content. Directly teaching that it is all right to feel content with where they are just now is often a very helpful de-stressor.
- *Show how advertising sells things by wrecking our contentment.* By making us aware of what we don't have and

making us think that we aren't as good unless we buy the product, advertisers are implying we aren't happy or content. An effective way of teaching children this is to make them contentment detectives on the lookout for things designed to make you feel like you don't have enough and you are lacking in some way. Once they are good at this with advertising and commercials, they can usually successfully extend this to discerning comments and actions in day-to-day life that ruin contentment.

7

Developing a Strong Teacher– Student Relationship

In the previous chapters, we set up a classroom to use a relationship-driven methodology. We made proactive moves to ensure that once filled with children, the classroom will engender positive and appropriate relationships.

It usually takes about 8 weeks for the relationship milieu to gel to a point that the relationships themselves become an integral part of motivation and change. The interim period tends to be taken up with getting acquainted, becoming familiar with the routine, setting and testing boundaries, and all the other normal aspects of adjusting to new experiences. If children are unfamiliar with healthy relationships, this is also a period when the teacher needs to focus on actively teaching relationship skills. After about eight weeks, the separate parts should start to show signs of coming together as a whole. That's our goal. We are trying to make a unit—a clan, as it were—out of all these different people. The magic of relationship methodology lies in the children's identifying themselves as a member of this particular clan in a way that ultimately helps them control their behavior.

There are many things we can do to encourage the formation of this unit and the accompanying sense of belonging. The logical place to begin is by actively strengthening the relationship between teacher and students.

First, it's important to always remember that as teacher we are the clan chieftain. We are not in an equal position to the other members of the group. This means we're not there to be our students' friend. They have the other kids for that role. Friendly, yes. We want to be friendly and approachable but at the same time never lose track of the fact that we are in charge. Leadership means we have extra obligations and responsibilities, as well as extra privileges, and we are a powerful role model. In tandem with this, we must keep in mind that we are also a teacher. So the way we lead our clan is by teaching.

While there are no "10 easy steps in relationship building," there are several concepts that can serve as guidelines for strengthening relationships between yourself and the students. The first important thing you need to realize is that you are there to teach the children how to behave functionally.

You Are There to Teach the Children how to Behave Functionally

The children in any special education class for behavior disorders are, by definition, going to exhibit significant dysfunctional behavior. In many instances, this dysfunctional behavior is the result of a maladaptive environment. In many instances, a destructive cycle has been put in motion where the child's dysfunction negatively impacts his or her environment, which in turn negatively impacts the child and creates more dysfunctional behavior. In most cases, the child will have experienced long-term or repeated dysfunctional relationships with adults.

As humans learn most adeptly through modeling, one of your primary tasks is to model how a functional adult behaves, how a functional adult relates to others, and how a functional adult handles negative situations. This shows the child what to expect from a healthy relationship and eventually how to take part in a relationship in a healthy and appropriate way herself. It also gives him or her firsthand experience of what it feels like to have a functional adult care about her.

To clarify what constitutes a *functional adult*, that is a person who should be able to do the following things with the child:

- Be fair
- Be moral
- Be honest
- Know his own strengths and weaknesses
- Know how to deal safely and effectively with his feelings
- Take responsibility for his own actions
- Show resilience
- Maintain a reasonable degree of optimism
- Behave consistently and predictably
- Recognize and respect boundaries
- Set boundaries in a way that is fair and appropriate
- Have realistic expectations of the child
- Endeavor to be firm, fair, and friendly all at the same time
- Take care of the child and not let her get into dangerous situations
- Help the child grow into the best person the child can be

THE CORNERSTONE OF RELATIONSHIPS IS TRUST

Because of repeated encounters with dysfunctional adults and a dysfunctional environment, children with behavioral disorders generally have serious problems with trust. As a consequence, trust needs to be one of the first issues addressed, as until children trust you to behave in a functional way, your effectiveness in using relationships as a medium of change is compromised. And until they trust the other children, there will be no formation of a cohesive unit.

Trust, like self-esteem, is not something that happens on demand. Don't be fooled by those hoary old exercises of falling backward into someone's arms. Trust is, in essence, simply feeling safe and secure in our environment. So it's earned, not engineered. You earn it by consistence. Once children feel safe in predicting your behavior, they will begin to trust. In the same way, they will begin to trust each other once they find the environment in the classroom is sufficiently consistent to feel safe, and you demonstrate you are consistently in control. With some children this will happen very quickly. Others may take weeks and weeks and are easily set back. A large part of the initial chaos is due to this lack of trust. Not sure the environment is safe, everyone has the tendency to test it, looking for the boundaries.

While modeling is crucial to establishing your trustworthiness, both as a functional adult and as the clan chieftain, it is helpful also to clarify for the children what trust is and what trustworthy behavior is by direct teaching.

When teaching about trust, remember the following:

- *Point out what people are doing in stories or real life,* and label the behavior as trustworthy or untrustworthy.
- *Actively teach how to be trustworthy.* Have children think of examples of trustworthy/untrustworthy behavior. Identify which things help us trust people, such as keeping your word, being fair, and being reliable.
- *Be extremely consistent* to encourage trust to develop between yourself and the children as quickly as possible. Consistency is *the* big issue. The reason we stop trusting people is because they are inconsistent. When we are among new people and in a new environment, it is normal to feel anxious and leery of being too trusting. Consistency eases these feelings more quickly.
- *Respond positively to the child in a way that shows genuine regard.* Smile. Greet the child when you see him or her. Try not to talk over a child or ignore him when talking to

someone else. Practice all the ordinary courtesies. Also, acknowledge efforts from the child to forge a bond, such as "Thank you for letting me know. It's hard to talk about things like this, but it helps me understand why. I want to know what is happening in your life."

- *Articulate worries you perceive the child having.* "By the way you are sitting, I sense that you feel bad about that. Can I help?" or "You don't look very happy today."
- *Articulate what you can be trusted not to do.* Many children from dysfunctional backgrounds have issues with adults regarding punishment, sexuality, or abandonment. Being very open about boundaries you, as a functional adult, will never cross is often very helpful in forming bonds. Say such things as "I am a safe adult. I never hit children when I am angry." On the other hand, *never* promise what you know you cannot deliver. Don't say, "You can trust me to always be here for you," because 10 years from now you and that child may not know each other.
- *Show your human side.* This engenders bonding because we tend to form relationships most easily with people we perceive are like us and therefore are most likely to understand us. Showing that you are human, just like the students, makes you more approachable and less intimidating. It also has the added benefit of modeling self-awareness for the children. Helpful ways to do this include the following:
  - o *Acknowledge your feelings.* "I feel frustrated when I see everybody out of their seat" or "I feel excited when it's time for art." If appropriate, talk through how you are handling your feelings. "I feel overwhelmed after all that concentrating. Going outside in the fresh air will make me feel better."
  - o *Acknowledge your physical state, particularly tiredness and stress.* By acknowledging you are tired or stressed, you make them aware of why people act differently in these states, but you also model how you handle it. You don't handle it by freaking out and throwing a chair across the room.

o *Talk about your experiences as a child of the same age.* Most children can't conceptualize adults as having been children. This allows the child to see you really have been there, and you really are capable of empathizing with them.

o *Talk about times you have done similar things as the child.* It is often deeply reassuring to children to know adults once behaved just like them and have still managed to go on to be good, respected, or successful people.

o *Take part in polls.* Virtually everyone enjoys polls, and they are enjoyable ways to find out more about each other. (Poll students, for example, on what the first five things are that they do when they wake up in the morning. Or who their favorite celebrity is. Or what animal they would choose to be.)

o *Share personal items such as photographs, particularly of yourself as a child.* This works well as part of a class project into personal history where everyone shares baby pictures or memories of being little.

o *Share ordinary events in their lives with the children occasionally.* Join them for lunch or playing playground games, for example.

And a last word: While sharing one's human side with the children is an important part of establishing and strengthening relationships, always do keep your boundaries as a functional adult clear. These boundaries will vary from person to person. Some teachers feel uncomfortable showing something as personal as a baby picture of themselves. That's fine. What we are striving for here is to be a warm, friendly, multidimensional person but also always a functional one, and this means respecting our own boundaries.

BE HONEST ABOUT CONSTRAINTS

Constraints are arbitrary boundaries. They are imposed by external parties, such as the school district, the government, or Mother Nature, and we have little or no control over them. Constraints will inevitably interfere from time to time, and it is important to acknowledge them and to teach the fine art of acceptance and/or letting go. Typical examples include the following:

- *Time constraints.* The school day is a given length. Often periods of study are preset.
- *Curriculum constraints.* Most teachers must follow a predetermined curriculum and administer standardized tests when instructed.
- *Financial constraints.* Most classrooms have very little money to spend.
- *Job constraints.* Certain behaviors, while in themselves are not inappropriate, aren't appropriate because of job constraints. For example, most teaching positions disallow taking a child home with you, even if you were to behave in a totally healthy and helpful way. Similarly, some teaching positions do not allow you to be alone with a student.

Don't make an issue of constraints, as this is offputting and usually deters trust, but always be honest with the children about the constraints being there. Otherwise, children may misinterpret constraints as your willfully choosing to pull back from them.

DISCIPLINE WITH FAIRNESS, HONESTY, AND COMPASSION

This is the place you will be most tested: those occasions when you have set limits, when you have had to stop something happening, or when you need to deal with meltdowns or the aftermath of serious misconduct. To prove you are a functional and trustworthy adult, you must be as fair, honest, and compassionate in these circumstances as you can manage. This means being willing to hear both sides of any argument no matter what you may already know, being open to the fact that there is always more than one way to interpret a situation, and avoiding actions that belittle, demean, or humiliate wrongdoers.

Ways to help maintain fair, honest, and compassionate discipline include the following:

- *Stay very focused on the process.* It is crucial to stay present when disciplining. Focus on the child, on the action, and on sorting it out *now.* Don't bring up old misbehaviors or make character judgments. If you need to link it to a chain of other misbehaviors, do so in a matter-of-fact manner rather than an accusatory, demeaning manner.

- *Attempt to see the situation from the other perspective.* Try to put yourself in the child's shoes and understand how the situation looked to her, or why she felt her action or reaction was necessary. Don't do this as a way of excusing the child but as a way of humanizing the action. This helps you to remain less judgmental and less inclined to humiliate or demean the child. Also, attempting to view the situation from the child's perspective allows you to understand better the genesis of the behavior and whether it was an approximation, a misunderstanding, an act of malice, sheer ignorance, or simply a slipup, as each of these requires a different response from you.

- *Deal with the immediate situation, but build in an opportunity to dissect it at a point when everyone is calmed down.* Emotions are usually running too high for any valuable, long-term learning to take place at the point when discipline is necessary. When everyone is calm, it is easier to hear both sides, correct any misperceptions, and teach prevention in the future. One of the best tools Torey found was to have the child write down his or her version of the incident and "mail" it to her in the suggestion box, the Kobold's Box, or the in tray on her desk. This allowed the child to express his feelings about the event, but the slowness of writing also tended to calm him down at the same time. They then arranged to talk about it at a later time, by which point everyone was generally calmer.

- *Reassure the child.* As the teacher, you are in a position of power, and thus, it's remarkably easy for children to take discipline very personally. Particularly early on in the relationship, they have a hard time distinguishing between discipline because they did something wrong and discipline because you hate them. Reassuring a child in the aftermath of discipline, particularly over big events, is important. Acknowledge openly that you genuinely like the child, that you are glad she is in your class, and that you understand how the event happened. Explain that it is your job to teach her how to behave in a better way, and you discipline because this is part of teaching her this, not because you dislike her personally. Reassure the child that you know she will eventually manage to control the behavior and, if at all possible (while still being honest) say that while this was a slipup, overall you really do think the child is doing better.

And finally, the biggie: Listen. If we had to sum the whole of the relationship-driven methodology up in one word, it's this: listen. Listen, listen, listen. It isn't a model at all, not really. It's just one action. And upon that one action, the whole methodology is based. To have a strong relationship with anyone, you must listen. Listen to the children when they talk to you. Stay right there in the moment and pay attention. Hear what *they* are saying, as opposed to what you think or want them to be saying, or as opposed to thinking about all the undone work or what you are supposed to pick up at the grocery store on the way home. The moment you manage to communicate in whatever manner you find best, be it your attitude, your posture, your words, your eye contact, or that you are fully present and genuinely listening to them, they will begin to trust you.

8

Preparing the Child for Successful Peer Relationships

I n a relationship-driven milieu, the interactions between the children are just as important to group cohesion as those between the teacher and the child. The biggest problem, however, is that children coming into a class for behavior disorders are very likely to have poor or inappropriate social skills as part of their etiology. Many will have difficulties making or keeping friends, and most will have had little experience of being a valued member of a cohesive, functional group. Our experience is that it is most productive just to assume poor social skills and to build teaching those skills directly into the curriculum from the onset.

SOCIAL SKILLS

It is important to help the children understand that social skills are such a vital part of being human that we continue to learn and refine them all our lives. Just a few examples of social skills are

- sharing;
- waiting one's turn;
- seeing another person's point of view;
- listening to others;
- helping others;
- taking part;
- empathizing and sympathizing;
- being respectful of other people, of their belongings, and of their beliefs; and
- using good manners.

Suggestions for teaching social skills include the use of games, role-playing, plays, Kobold's Box, and social stories.

- Games are a highly valuable social skills tool, and they have the advantage of making things more fun at the same time. Incorporate games—both individual child-to-child or teacher-to-child games and group/team games. We found it generally more effective to choose the teams ourselves in order to make sure they were balanced in terms of abilities and that no one was made to feel unpopular. Actively teach good sportsmanship skills but also teach the children to recognize which behaviors make team members feel unpopular or unwanted and why we choose not to act that way toward other players, whatever their skill level. This is an inordinately valuable time to teach group cohesiveness. Vary the games. Use some which rely totally on cooperation and others that allow competitiveness. Games analysis, developed by G. S. Don Morris (Morris & Stiehl, 1999), is a helpful method for designing group/team games to accommodate children's individual social, emotional, and motoric development.
- Mike and Torey's favorite way of directly teaching social skills was role-playing. This method is highly beneficial as it allows the child to rehearse what he or she is going

to do, which decreases social anxiety. But it also gives you and the class an opportunity to provide feedback and constructive criticism in a way that is nonthreatening.

- With plays, children can practice social skills using their imagination and creativity. Put the children in groups and allow them to make up a short skit around a particular social skill. For example, the scenario might be that you are walking down the street, and you see someone slip and fall. The children create the scene and then explain why they chose the actions they did. More elaborate examples can be captured with a video camera and become a complete production.

- Kobold's Box is another imaginative means of teaching social skills. As Torey described in detail with Sheila's class, she used the story of the kobold, a little gnome in the classroom who put notes in a wooden box whenever he noticed someone doing something helpful, and then Torey encouraged the children to add their own notes when they noticed others behaving well.

- *Social stories* are carefully crafted stories designed specifically for children on the autistic spectrum but useful also with very shy children and others with markedly low social skills. The stories contain a series of sentences (descriptive, directive, perspective, affirmative, cooperative, and control) that aim to give the child clear, understandable information about different social situations.

These are general social skills. However, we've found that there are four special social areas which are often troublesome for children in special education. To help them get the most out of peer relationships in a relationship-driven milieu, it is helpful to target these areas and teach directly to the children. They are

- how to make friends,
- how to self-assess,
- how to problem solve, and
- how to cope with conflicts.

MAKING FRIENDS

Most children in classes for behavioral disorders are socially isolated. They usually have low self-esteem and are poor at reading body language or nonverbal cues. This makes them appear awkward or inappropriate. Many go blundering uncomprehendingly into situations they can't read well, and most worry that others don't like them or that they will be humiliated, overwhelmed, or unable to cope in social situations. To complicate matters, most have limited access to normal social settings, as they often don't participate in child-oriented, extracurricular activities like Scouts, sports, dance, and the like. Thus, it is helpful to be very clear about what goes into being friendly. Opening or closing circle is a good time to have this discussion or to review these points. Children usually enjoy brainstorming the concept themselves.

Making friends falls into two parts, the initial stage of meeting someone new and the follow-up stage of maintaining a friendship.

Meeting Someone New: Breaking the Ice

Children can find meeting new people less daunting if they are shown friendships begin in a series of incremental steps:

1. *Smile.* People are more likely to be friendly to someone with a nice look on their face.

2. *Make eye contact.* This shows you have noticed them and are paying attention to them.

3. *Greet the other person.*

4. *Ask a polite question.* Help children understand that small talk is nothing more than a series of polite objective questions or comments, *not* about yourself, that show you are interested in the other person and want to know more about them. Explain that this is a great way to find

out if you have anything in common, but you need to be careful not to grill them. Sometimes we use small talk just to show we are friendly, and on those occasions we are usually talking about something both we and the other person are experiencing, like waiting in line or the weather. From a developmental perspective, though children start out very egocentric and must learn how to see other points of view, most younger children or those with developmental delays will need help mastering small talk because they have trouble understanding how to talk about something other than themselves or their own interests. It helps to directly teach it and practice it through role-play. Workable small talk topics include

- o TV and popular culture (e.g., What shows do you like?),
- o activities (e.g., What do you like to do after school?),
- o noticing something about the person and politely asking about it (e.g., I like your shirt. Is it new? or Your pencil case is nice. Where did you get it?), and
- o asking an opinion about an experience they are both sharing (e.g., What do you think of the new gym? or Did you like the lunch today?).

5. *Listen.* Pay attention when the other person is talking. Good friends listen to each other instead of talking over one another or planning what they each will say next. Listening also gives you important information about what the person thinks and knows, and this makes it easier for you to know what to say next.

6. *Think about the other person instead of yourself.* Focus on what they are saying, what they are feeling, and what may be interesting to them. This makes you appear friendlier. The bonus is that it keeps you from feeling anxious, because anxiety happens when we are thinking about ourselves.

Keeping Your Friend

Tell your students that maintaining friendships isn't hard if they can remember these tips:

- *Be yourself.* You don't have to be someone different. You're good enough as you are, and friends will know this.
- *Be helpful.* Doing little things shows that you care.
- *Listen.* Being a friend means you don't do all the talking.
- *Don't boast or show off.* Being a friend means you don't worry about being better than they are.
- *Laugh and have fun together.* A fun person is fun to be with, but only laugh with your friends and not at them.
- *Be trustworthy.* Friends don't tell each other's secrets or gossip about each other or go behind each other's back. Friends don't lie to each other.
- *Be loyal.* Friends stick up for each other and help each other out when there are problems.
- *Be tolerant.* Being a friend means you aren't judgmental or critical. If a friend is doing something wrong, you try to help them do better without making them feel bad.
- *Be respectful.* Being a friend means you don't insult each other or put each other down. You don't try to control how the other person acts, looks, or talks, but let him make his own decisions about himself.
- *Be understanding.* A friend is someone who understands you. If you and your friend have a disagreement, try to understand what happened. If your friend has a bad experience, difficult day, or something similar, show sympathy and be reassuring.

SELF-ASSESSMENT

Self-assessment, also called self-efficacy, is the ability to accurately assess one's own thoughts and actions. It is closely related to self-awareness and the ability to see things from another perspective insofar as it requires the ability to look at oneself objectively. This is an ongoing process for us all, and most of us will continue developing self-awareness and refining our self-assessment skills all our lives.

Self-assessment plays a critical role in a relationship-driven classroom, because this is how one catches and corrects one's own misbehavior. It is important children know what self-assessment is and learn how to go about it realistically. As they practice this skill, responsibility for monitoring behavior slowly shifts away from the teacher to the child and, ultimately, to internal control.

Teaching self-assessment can be managed several ways:

- *Regularly use phrases to encourage self-assessment,* both positive and negative. Take time to listen to answers and give feedback, such as
  - "How did you think you did on that?"
  - "What needs more work?"
  - "What did you do well?"
  - "What was your weakest point?"
  - "What's your best feature?"
- *Make it clear that we self-assess in order to change what isn't working.* It isn't about feeling embarrassed or ashamed because we did something wrong. It's about finding out what the problems are so that we can solve them.
- *Thoroughly discuss the difference between self-assessment and self-judgment.* Assessment is based on our actions, and actions usually produce external, objective evidence. A test result, for example, is an assessment because anyone looking at it can see what has been assessed. Judgment is based on our feelings and feelings are usually internal and subjective, and no one except the person herself can know what her feelings are. "I'm stupid" is a judgment, for example.

  Most children will need quite a lot of practice separating these two. Show how, for example, "I'm stupid" is different from "I failed that test," because "I'm stupid" isn't based on an action, so we can't know what to change. "I failed that test" *is* an action, so we can figure out ways to do it differently next time so that we don't fail.

- *Correct misconceptions.* Self-assessment only works if it is accurate. If the child wildly misguesses or if his self-image is so low that he regularly underestimates himself, clarify and help him reassess a situation until it is more accurate.

PROBLEM-SOLVING TECHNIQUES

Problems are going to arise. This is a natural part of life. Many children with behavior disorders respond very chaotically when confronted with problems. Others give up immediately. Most show little perseverance. Consequently, we've found it very useful to teach children directly that problems, whatever they might be, tend to have patterns and because of this, it is usually possible to approach a problem and solve it in a concrete, step-by-step way.

Our basic step-by-step outline for problem solving looks like this:

1. Wait until you are calm before trying to solve a problem.

2. Make sure you understand what the problem is before you do anything.

3. Restate the problem in your own words. This helps you understand it.

4. Look at it from all sides. Try to see other perspectives if other people are involved before you do anything.

5. If you can't see the other person's point of view; talk it over with someone else who is understanding but objective,

6. Most problems have patterns, so look for the pattern; for example,

- o Does it always start at the same time of day, such as when it's time to line up or at the beginning of recess?
- o Does it always start when you are tired, hungry, or cold?
- o Does it always start when there are two vowels together in a word, or when there are fractions, or when you are using art materials?
- o Does it always start when you are feeling left out, on your own, or angry?

7. It's usually easier to solve problems if we can use different senses. Try approaching the problem differently:

- o Write it down if you've been talking about it.
- o Try drawing a picture, a map, or a diagram of a problem to give visual clues. If you using your eyes to look at the problem, try turning away and having someone describe it to you or talk to you about it, so that you can hear it.
- o If you are reading it, try talking to someone about it.

8. *Be okay with making mistakes.* Good problem solvers always make lots of mistakes. These aren't failures. They're "tries." It's okay to have lots of tries when solving a problem.

9. *Don't get frustrated.* It's important to know the following:

- o It's hard to come up against something you don't understand and you don't know how to solve (That's why it's called a problem!).
- o Everyone feels like this.

If you get frustrated, it makes you lose your concentration, and that makes the problem harder to solve. Take a deep breath if you feel yourself getting frustrated, or take a break away from the problem. Walk away from it a while.

10. *Don't get anxious.*

   o It's natural to feel worried about something you don't understand and you don't know how to solve. (That's why it's called a problem!)
   o Everyone feels like that.

   If you get worried, it makes you lose your concentration, and that makes the problem harder. Again, take a deep breath, if you begin to feel anxious. Take a break away from the problem. Walk away or leave it for a while.

11. *If you lose your concentration, it is most helpful to take a break.* If you can't see any solutions, leaving the problem alone lets your other mind work on it, and when you come back to it, you will usually see the problem with fresh eyes. This makes it easier to see patterns and solutions.

12. *Keep track of things you have tried.* It's easy to go through a lot of possible solutions that don't work and then get confused as to what's been tried and what hasn't. Keeping track of your tries stops this from happening and helps others who might come later to solve the problem. Writing the tries down is usually the easiest way to keep track.

Other helpful techniques to incorporate in problem solving are the following:

   • *Practice problem-solving techniques using puzzles, games, and stories,* like Encyclopedia Brown, that are just slightly harder than the group can do. Solve the problems as a group and focus on the step-by-step process of problem solving rather than on the solution. In other words, reinforce the children for tackling the problem systematically as outlined above instead of for getting the answer. This allows the slower children to participate equally and helps them understand the individual components of problem solving more clearly.

- *Talk through real-life problems you as a teacher encounter in the classroom, as you, yourself, solve them.* Be as transparent as possible in your own problem-solving techniques so that the children can see problem solving in action. Torey can remember one occasion where they were hurrying as a group to get ready for a class photograph that was being taken in the room. Just before the photographer arrived, one child accidentally knocked a box off one of the tables. It was absolutely full of small LEGO pieces, and they went everywhere. This was back in the era when most children came to school in special or new clothes for the photograph, and Torey just couldn't cope with having everyone crawling around on the floor in their good clothes, retrieving a million bits of LEGO pieces. She told everyone to "freeze" and then said just to leave it until after the photograph, which they did. Afterward, she talked very specifically about having chosen to leave the toys and go ahead with the picture, because when it first happened she felt very annoyed, and she needed to be calm first. This time gave her space to think about what to do. She then talked about what the problem was: how to pick up all the pieces of Lego without everyone getting their clothes dirty. Saying, "This happened, and I did this in response, because . . ." on a regular basis gives the children a real chance to see problem solving carried out in a functional, organized way.
- *Deconstruct successfully handled problems.* Similarly, if you see a child dealing with a problem in a positive and effective way, ask her to talk about what she did. Quite often the child will find it somewhat challenging to articulate, so help her put it into order. Most children are pleased by this sort of attention, and helping them organize and articulate their behavior gives them a better perspective of their positive actions.
- *Use problems presented in popular TV shows and in books to illustrate how the characters went through the problem-solving behavior described earlier to reach their solutions.* Many

sitcoms revolve around really poor problem-solving skills and the difficulties the character gets into as a result. Watching clips of these and analyzing why things got confused or went wrong can be a very effective way of teaching problem solving. Very old sitcoms such as *I Love Lucy* and *Leave It to Beaver* are particularly good for this, as the story lines tend to be very transparent and rely heavily on literal or slapstick humor, so it is easy for the children to understand what is happening and antici-pate the results. The absurdity of poor problem solving, which is also what gives it its comedic value, often stays with the children more effectively than straightforward lessons.

CONFLICT MANAGEMENT AND RESOLUTION TECHNIQUES

A major part of the day in the average class for children with behavior disorders involves conflict. To make a relationship-driven milieu work, we as teachers need to be able to manage and de-escalate conflict effectively. But for children to perma-nently change their behavior, as opposed to just having us con-trol it, they too need to understand how conflicts work and how to go about dealing with them effectively.

It is helpful to start by directly teaching that when a conflict happens, there are three possible ways we can respond: with aggression, avoidance, or problem solving.

Aggression

Conflict occurs and we feel angry or upset, so we attack the other person either physically or verbally to show them how angry or upset we are. Typical examples of dealing with con-flicts by aggression are hitting, fighting, name-calling, throwing things, and going to war.

The problem with this way of responding to a conflict is that it never resolves anything, even if there is a temporary winner. The conflict usually escalates until one party hurts the other too badly for it to continue. When the conflict stops, the defeated side often feels angry and wants revenge, so the conflict is likely to continue below the surface and then flare up again at a later time.

Avoidance

Conflict occurs and we feel angry or upset, but instead of saying what bothers us, we pretend there is no problem. We pretend we aren't angry or upset, or we show we are upset but refuse to talk about it or be around the other person. Typical examples of avoidance behavior as a way of dealing with conflicts are the silent treatment of someone or walking off in a huff.

The problem with this way of responding to a conflict is that other people do not know what is wrong. Because they can't see inside our heads, they do not know why we are angry. Consequently, it is unlikely they will behave different the next time or that they will feel good about themselves or us when the conflict is over.

Problem Solving

Conflict occurs and we feel angry or upset, so we talk about what happened without insulting or blaming each other to try and see what went wrong. If we are feeling very strongly, we walk away for a while and cool down first. Both sides acknowledge they have a difference that is causing hurt feelings or anger. They then sit down together and think of ways to solve it. Finally, they choose a solution that works best for everyone.

Why this works: After resolving a conflict with problem solving, people tend to feel positive and understood, even if the solution ends up being different than they wanted. They are more likely to remember the solution the next time the problem occurs.

It is very, very helpful for children to become thoroughly familiar with these three forms of response to conflict, because the more familiar they are, the more easily they will recognize avoidance or aggression happening in their own conflicts. This awareness is what will eventually provide them with that crucial moment of space before reacting that will allow them to choose an alternate behavior, such as problem solving.

The very best teaching tool in our experience has been role-playing. Most kids thoroughly enjoy re-acting conflict of any sort. Using circle time or a specified curriculum time to act out various types of conflicts and various types of response to conflicts provides good practice for when real conflicts come along. Most children enjoy role-playing negative emotions, and this can often evoke good conversations about the feelings going on inside when conflict occurs.

It is also effective to look back on previous experiences that didn't work out and troubleshoot them. For general teaching of conflict management, it is better not to pick out one or two students as examples, as this type of highlighting of negative behavior for everyone's benefit isn't helpful to the self-esteem of the one or two. Instead, use instances where the whole class experiences negative responses to conflict. For example, if there is conflict over who gets to use a certain instrument say, "When I bring out the instruments, there is a lot of fighting over who gets to do what first. What's happening? How can we get this to work better?"

Indeed, it is occasionally helpful to stop kids right in the midst of real conflicts and have them act out a better response, or act out the response they were giving as role-play. Suddenly seeing the conflict as a role-play instead of from the inside often provides children enough space to see where the difficulties lie and what is a better response. The aggro value of being stopped in the middle of being mad to do playacting is also effective!

As well as teaching conflict management and resolution techniques, it is helpful to directly teach the kinds of behaviors that specifically escalate conflicts and de-escalate them, because many children will not be able to make the logical leap from the three responses to conflict.

BEHAVIORS THAT ESCALATE CONFLICTS

Attacking Behaviors

Aggression, whether it is physical, verbal, or emotional, virtually always makes situations worse. Initially it may feel good as pent-up emotions are released, and it is important to acknowledge this component of aggressive behavior, because many children will be used to reacting simply to experience this release and they don't think much further. Examples of attacking behaviors are

- hitting, kicking, spitting, and shoving;
- name calling, teasing, taunting, gossiping, accusing;
- using "you" messages, such as "You always get us in trouble" or "You really make me mad"; and
- using judgmental language such as *should, ought,* and *must* or their negatives, along with *never, always,* and *can't,* which often appear in conjunction with "you" messages, such as "You always wreck our fun" or "You shouldn't do that."

Avoiding Behaviors

Avoidance is a trickier concept than aggression. Avoiding facing the problem will, in the long term, always prolong or escalate a conflict, and when it becomes a primary way of dealing with conflicts, it can be a very unhelpful behavior indeed. However, there are times when avoidance is the right choice in the short term. It is important to discuss this area thoroughly with children so that they understand it is all right to avoid situations where personal safety is involved and that if a problem feels bigger than they can sort out themselves, it is better to avoid it temporarily and get help to resolve it rather than get in too deep. Examples of avoidance behaviors include

- refusing to talk,
- ignoring, and
- running away.

Cornering Behaviors

Actions that make people feel cornered by a situation escalate a conflict because they produce feelings of fear and desperation. When people are frightened, they are more likely to be unpredictable. When they feel desperate they are more likely to do dangerous things they wouldn't do otherwise. Examples of cornering behaviors are

- standing too close or leaning over someone,
- using intense eye contact,
- insisting the other person respond in a precise way,
- making threats, and
- saying or implying the other person cannot leave, get away, or otherwise return to normal activities.

Jumping to Conclusions

Assuming we know what another person is thinking or feeling escalates a conflict because in this mind-set, we don't listen. We think we already have the answer. Not only are jumped-to conclusions often just plain incorrect because we are judging the situation only from our own perspective; they are also demeaning to the other person by not allowing him or her to speak for him- or herself.

Issuing Challenges

Words don't necessarily have to be attacking or accusatory to escalate speech. Challenges are something most kids don't think consciously about at all, so it is very helpful for them to become aware of making challenges. Most verbal challenges are simply open-ended statements phrased as a question; for example,

- So? So what?
- You gonna make me?
- What are you looking at?

Being Disrespectful

Hostile body language or tone of voice escalates conflict. Examples of this are

- sarcastic tone,
- critical tone,
- sighing,
- rolling eyes,
- arms crossed, and
- impatient tapping.

Not Sticking to the Issues

When a conflict happens, it is very tempting to bring up old disagreements, infringements, mistakes, and other detritus.

BEHAVIORS THAT DE-ESCALATE CONFLICT

Stop, Look, and Listen

Most conflicts happen because we're not aware of what we're doing or what others are doing, and we rush headlong forward. Teach the children that the road-crossing code works well here too. Stop and become aware of what you are feeling inside and of what you are doing. Look at the problem at hand. And listen to what the other person has to say before you start talking.

Respectful Behaviors

Actions that make others feel like we take them seriously as a person, that we are listening to them, and that we care about what they think and feel are respectful behaviors. Ways we show this are by

- listening to the other person without interrupting,
- monitoring our tone of voice or using a soft tone of voice,
- keeping an open or relaxed body posture, and
- not speaking for or about other people.

Conciliatory Language

Certain ways of talking make people feel better about us and encourage them to talk with us; the following are examples:

- Use "I" messages when talking about the problem, such as "I feel mad about this right now" or "I don't like it when you take my things" instead of the accusatory "you" messages.
- Use reflective listening or rephrasing what you hear the other person saying so that if he says, "You make me mad," you respond with "You're feeling mad now." Or she says, "He took the last cookie," and you respond with "You wanted the last cookie, and now he's taken it." Reflective listening is useful for us to do because it helps us make sure we *are* listening instead of planning our own next response. It also reassures the other person his thoughts and feelings have been heard.
- Use neutral responses. Most challenging or escalating responses are open-ended questions. In contrast, most neutral responses are closed statements; for example,
  o "I hear what you're saying" or "I know what you mean."
  o "Thank you for letting me know how you feel."
  o "I can see you feel strongly about that."
  o "Those are interesting ideas."

Stay Focused on the Issue at Hand

Don't bring up older unresolved issues or past misbehavior. Other or older issues can be discussed at another time. When deescalating a conflict, stick just to the problem causing the present conflict.

Try to See the Other Point of View

Understandably, this is hard to do when you are feeling angry or upset with someone, but it is the single most effective way to deescalate a conflict and, indeed, to defray future conflicts because it engenders understanding. With practice, it can be incorporated into stop, look, and listen.

Avoid Humiliating the Other Person

Many times conflicts can only be resolved when one person admits she is wrong or she is declared wrong by someone in authority. If we allow the person to save face, she is more likely to accept the resolution positively, and the conflict is permanently resolved. This is a complex concept that is developmentally beyond younger children. To directly teach it, encourage the children to think about how it feels when you are wrong about something and someone lords it over you or makes you feel stupid, and work back from there (e.g., how could someone behave toward you that would be more helpful?). It takes a lot of practice to understand this, but it is worth the time.

Take a Time-Out

Sometimes our emotions are just running too high to do any of the above. Teach the children to recognize this point and to understand that when they reach it, usually the best action is to give themselves a time-out, though not in a negative way. Explain that the real idea behind a time-out is not punishment but rather to give us time to calm down and get back in control of ourselves. This is an appropriate, helpful thing to do, and it works both ways. Sometimes we find that we are able to maintain our cool during a conflict but the other person isn't. So it is helpful to suggest a time-out to cool down before resuming efforts to resolve the conflict. Typical ways we can indicate a time-out is to say things such as the following:

- "I'm going to count to ten, so that I don't get angry."
- "Let's take a break and cool down."
- "I'll talk to you when I'm calmer."
- "Give me a chance to sleep on this, and we'll talk about it tomorrow."
- "I'll talk to you when you're feeling less angry."

Using these pointers, it is easy to develop a step-by-step outline for conflict resolution that suits your particular classroom, similar to the one given for problem solving.

The basic outline can be reduced right down to stop, look, and listen:

1. *Stop:* Take a deep breath. Are you calm enough to continue? If not, take a break until you feel calmer and then come back to the issue.

2. *Look:* (1) Look at what the problem is and stay on just that issue. Don't bring other things into it. (2) Look forward to what can be done to sort things out, not back at what has happened and can't be changed. (3) Look at the other person's point of view.

3. *Listen:* Listen to what each other is saying and say back what you hear him or her saying to make sure you've understood it correctly. Each person has the right to express his or her side of the issue without being attacked, challenged, or humiliated. We take it in turn to speak and to listen to what the other person is saying.

9

Successful Group Dynamics

What sets the relationship-driven methodology apart from other methodologies is its active use of interpersonal relationships as a medium for change. Thus far we've focused primarily on individual relationships—those between teacher and child and those among the children. But there is also a third force: the group or unit relationship, or, in other words, belonging.

Being part of a group is an important facet of being human. We are social creatures by nature. When we feel disconnected from others, we are unhappy, lonely, and depressed. In contrast, a life rich in social connection lends itself to feelings of happiness and fulfillment. So, one of our main roles as teachers in the relationship-driven classroom is to foster strong interpersonal bonds with the children, and at the same time a sense of the class as a single unit. This provides a crucial sense of connection for the students. For the teacher, it provides a very efficient means for both motivation and discipline.

CONCRETE IDENTIFICATION

Helping children identify themselves as part of the class needs to begin on a concrete level—things that children can see, hear, and identify as signifying the group. It also needs to be done with sensitivity. Many children coming into the class will not initially want to be there. Being identified as in this particular group may have negative connotations that may be further reinforced at home or on the playground. Be sensitive to this, and avoid class identifiers that can be ridiculed or make the child stand out elsewhere. This is particularly true early in the school year. As the group becomes cohesive and confident, they may flaunt their special status shamelessly with all sorts of signs and symbols, and that's fine, but leave that decision to them. In the beginning, be subtle, and keep these concrete identifiers within the classroom.

Things that work at this stage are classroom symbols, inclusive language, group homilies, and special group activities.

Classroom Symbols

Torey found it very helpful to have a single, small, and specific symbol that stood for their class. She usually started with something discreet—a red dot, for example. She then stuck this on all the books, on all the transportable classroom belongings but also on name tags, messages to the office, and on anything else concerning her class. Torey used it with all classroom communication as well, including things like the class rules posted on the board. This kind of concrete identifier quickly allowed children to see what belonged to the classroom, and as it was also on their notebooks, workbooks, and other materials, they quickly identified as being in this group too.

Once Torey's class was established, they often then designed a new class symbol together. It still works best to keep this quite simple, as it is most effective if it can be made into stickers, buttons, and so forth. Alternately, if her original symbol was something that she'd affixed to things like classroom textbooks, it wasn't very practical to change this latterly. In that case, they designed a class flag or coat of arms. One year involved a very elaborate papier-mâché version of their classroom coat of arms that all the children worked on together, both designing and slapping on the papier-mâché, and they hung it over the door for the remainder of the year.

Inclusive Language

Use the language of unity. Speak in the royal "we." Frequently identify the group both as a group and as belonging to you, using such statements as "You're part of my group" or "You're with me" or "We're together in this."

Group Homilies

Make a few phrases your own. Language is a powerful way to create group identification. Regularly repeated phrases create an affectionate shared "family history" among the group ("Miss Hayden *always* says that!"). These phrases can also provide useful mnemonic devices for behavior ("What do we always say in here?"), which include the child at the same time as reminding her of appropriate behavior. The phrases can also be extended to work as a secret code outside the classroom. Having the children know when they are away from the classroom that if you say certain phrases, you want special behavior can be very useful, and the inclusiveness of the secret code aspect often appeals far more than simply demanding the behavior.

Choose simple, easy-to-remember phrases that encourage desired behaviors such as "You haven't failed as long as you're still trying" or "Hard is not impossible." However, do think the phrases through. Some popular adages, such as "there's no such word as can't," tend to be discouraging to those who are struggling, because the adages aren't really true. And never use these homilies against a child or as a means of excluding him or her from the group if he or she misbehaves.

Some people enjoy using humorous exclamations ("Oh snickerdoodle!") as part of their group language, and this works well if you have the natural dramatic flair to pull it off. We find, however, it's a fine line between a humorous phrase and a silly phrase. Most people can consciously add a couple of adages to their classroom vocabulary and sound warm and inclusive, but exclamatory phrases can bring us dangerously close to sounding like Ned Flanders in *The Simpsons*.

Special Group Activities

Establish early on a few positive activities that are fun and specific to your class, as well as being useful for teaching skills. This helps offset the negative stereotype of the special education class as well as providing a good group bonding opportunity. Examples from Torey's classrooms include the following:

- *Cooking:* She set 30 minutes to an hour aside each Wednesday afternoon to make food or occasionally playthings from kitchen materials, such as crazy putty or playdough. This is a wonderful activity for teaching many group-appropriate behaviors such as sharing, taking turns, and cooperation, as well as more traditional educational subjects like math and reading.

- *The Kobold's Box:* She came up with the Kobold's Box in an effort to reinforce positive behavior in her classroom, but the fact that the kobold visited just their room at the school turned it into one of the special treats for being in her classroom. Pointing out to the children the things that are special just to them helps cement group identification.

- *Friday afternoon treats:* In several classes they "celebrated being us" by giving over 15 to 30 minutes on Friday afternoons to planned treats and group activities. One class opted for Hershey bars and board games, for example. Another opted for music and puzzles. A third wanted story time and a chance to put on plays.

De-Emphasizing Comparisons

The single most damaging thing to group unity is the comparison of one member to another. This shifts the focus from the group as a whole to the individuals within it, and it is always divisive because it implies that some members are more valuable than others. It is also counterproductive. The depreferenced child takes a self-esteem hit, and the preferenced child is encouraged to crave the approval of others. When we are trying to form a cohesive group, we want all members to feel equally valued, and this is most easily done by recognizing each of us is different with unique strengths and weaknesses, so any comparison ends up being between apples and oranges, and thus serves no purpose.

Nonetheless, we are judgmental creatures by habit, so it is important to confront this issue openly and straightforwardly. The teacher needs to explain the concept of each individual as unique to the class, not only because children may not be used to thinking this way themselves, but also because they won't be expecting you to think this way. They will tend to perceive slights and judgments because they are expecting them, and it takes direct teaching before they learn to think this other way. The following are ways to avoid comparisons between individuals:

- *Actively teach the children not to compare with each other.* Squash comparison words when you hear them. Explain comparing isn't helpful because each of us is unique, and so we are never able to compare exactly the same thing between two people.
- *Actively teach the only valid comparison is with oneself.* The person the child should compare herself against is who she was previously. This is how we know we have grown. Keep charts so that children can see their own progress. Also keep folders of earlier work as the year passes so that children can compare how they have done. *This* is healthy comparison and will always stimulate self-esteem without damaging group cohesiveness.

- *There is a difference between competition and comparison.* When we compare, it is about people: "He is smarter than John is" or "Why can't you be more like Sally?" When we compete, it is about actions: a faster speed, a higher score, or a winning game. The following methods actively teach the components of healthy competition:
  - o *It is confined to one setting.* Competition is limited. It lasts for the length of the Monopoly game or the track meet or the spelling bee. Then it is over, and we stop thinking of the other person as a competitor, a winner, or a loser and go back to thinking of him as a friend whom we care about.
  - o *It is confined to actions.* Competition is about being able to do something better than others. Doing is an action. Actions are things we can change, so this is why we can work at getting better and competing again.
- *Teach the skills that allow children to respond appropriately in competitive situations.* Among these skills are
  - o having good sportsmanship;
  - o being a gracious loser, because it is about your actions and not you, and maybe next time you will win;
  - o being a gracious winner and not boasting or lording it over others, because it is about your actions and not you, and maybe next time you will lose;
  - o using self-assessment: how to judge your actions; and
  - o using self-encouragement: how to cheer yourself on to try your hardest when things get tough, how to remind yourself that losing happens to all of us, and what's important is trying your best.

GROUP RESPONSIBILITY

One of the most important differences between a cohesive community and a disparate crowd is that in the community, individuals take responsibility for one another. Consequently, one of the most powerful ways of making the class cohesive is to actively encourage children to be responsible for other

members of the class as well as themselves. This isn't a particularly well-known concept in our culture, where emphasis is on
individualism and self-reliance, but it is nonetheless a valuable
concept and extremely helpful in generating both motivation
and self-control in the classroom.

Ways to directly teach group responsibility include the
following:

- *Practice Chinese happiness or shadowing.* The legend is that
  in Chinese families, the eldest child was responsible for
  the happiness of the next eldest child in the family, and
  that child was responsible for the happiness of the next
  child, and so on. This process of actively making one child
  responsible for the well-being of another child works well
  in small doses in the classroom. It can be worked one of
  two ways. In the first, the child draws or is given a name
  and he is that person's *happiness elf* (or whatever name
  you give it) for the rest of the morning or other specified
  time. The child tries to do what he can to be helpful and
  kind to that person. This is effective in encouraging the
  child to be sensitive to someone else's well-being, but
  it is a sufficiently artificial setup that it needs to be time
  limited. It works best if it is a regularly occurring thing so
  that the children get used to the idea and the activity. The
  other way is to simply assign one child to another as that
  child's shadow. The shadow is the helper, and her job is to
  look out for the person she is shadowing and be the one
  that child can turn to if he has problems. This works well
  as a long-term way of fostering responsibility for each
  other. It needs to be closely monitored in the beginning,
  however, especially if shadows have social skills issues
  such as autism, as it takes practice to see when someone
  else needs help and how to offer it appropriately. But once
  the children get used to it, most are quite good at shadowing and at helping each other shadow.
- *Help others in order to reach a common goal.* Inevitably
  there are those occasions where everyone wants to do

something but one or two members hold the entire group up. These situations, which have such potential to cause division and argument, are also absolute gold for fostering group responsibility. Help children become aware that they will reach the goal faster if they take responsibility for assisting those who need it, rather than getting angry with them or putting them down. Discuss strategies of how to divide responsibility. In one class, for example, the two youngest could not tie their shoelaces, and this always held the students up coming into the classroom and going out. So instead of everyone standing around impatiently, two of the older boys accepted responsibility for tying the younger ones' laces and, eventually, for teaching them how to do it themselves.

An alternate form of this is to make some activities possible only if the whole group succeeds or cooperates. Children will need help initially in carrying this out without becoming negative toward members of the class who are struggling with the activity, and they will need help understanding the difference between assisting a fellow member of the group to achieve something and doing the task for him. In the beginning when teaching this concept, it is best to use enjoyable, nonacademic tasks such as jigsaw puzzles or baking where everyone can join in but no one feels pressured by performance. Once the children have mastered the general concepts of group activity, you can move on to academics.

- *Peer tutoring.* This is closely related to the above insofar as once children understand the concept of group activities, it becomes quite natural for the older or more skilled ones to help the younger or less skilled. Assigning children to do this often strengthens group bonds, increases self-esteem of both the tutor and the child being helped, and provides a valuable template for success in general group activities, as children will more naturally think of helping those who are struggling.

- *Group punishment.* Yes, we know this is a very unpopular concept today, and certainly it is unfair on those occasions where there is only one miscreant who acted alone or in an unstoppable manner, such as a rage. However, there are also occasions when a significant number of children are misbehaving or there is minor misbehavior going on that everyone knows shouldn't be happening. Group punishment shouldn't be a regular occurrence in the class, but it can serve as a good means of helping children perceive they are interconnected, if used judiciously. Our rationale to the kids is "Yes, it would be unfair if it were just about you, if you were being punished for something you didn't do, but this is about the group. And you are part of the group. Being part of the group means you are responsible for helping everyone to behave or complete work or whatever. If you see someone acting out or falling behind, then you need to help them. But no one was helping this time, so everyone is guilty."
- *Be absolutely unequivocal about bullying.* Bullying is intentionally intimidating weaker people, and it is seriously destructive to group cohesion, so it is paramount that you deal immediately and decisively with any signs of it. Do not let stronger members of the group *ever* victimize weaker members. Pecking-order behavior will happen as a natural part of group dynamics, particularly in the beginning. Keep a close eye on it, and correct it any time it strays into harassment or maltreatment (and punish it, if necessary).

Much of the time bullying will appear as a normal part of boundary testing. If you are firm and clear about what is acceptable in your classroom and what is not, the children usually settle down quite quickly and bullying disappears. However, there is always going to be the occasional career bully, that kid who persistently picks on others. With these children, it is important to keep in mind this whole philosophy of "no one chooses to be unhappy." This is a teaching opportunity. Recognize the child is behaving in this manner because he hasn't landed on a more productive way to manage his self-esteem or interact with others. Be absolutely strict about not allowing bullying, but do show understanding toward the bully, and focus on helping him learn more appropriate and rewarding social behaviors.

GROUP PROBLEM SOLVING

One of the most useful ways of unifying a group is to solve problems together. This not only brings a democratic feel to what is actually a benign autocracy, but facing problems together is an important bonding activity. It also allows you to model and teach problem solving and conflict resolution in an organized, step-by-step fashion that can then serve as a template for other settings. In directly teaching group problem solving, it is best to do the following:

- *Do it regularly.* To be effective, group problem solving needs to be a done frequently enough that everyone becomes comfortable both with the format and with each other's approach to problems. Facing small, ordinary problems daily is more successful than facing the occasional bigger, more interesting or more thought-provoking problem. Torey used opening and closing circle as their regular problem solving and conflict resolution forum. Sometimes her class worked on problems that were giving them trouble, such as "What can we do about the problem we're have with people using things that don't belong to them without asking first?" Sometimes they worked on general issues that Torey provided: "How would you handle overhearing someone say something bad about someone else here in the group?" And sometimes the group solved fun problems such as "If we had a million dollars to spend on going somewhere together, how would we decide where to go?"

Once the children become accustomed to solving problems as a group, make use of spontaneous problem solving and conflict resolution opportunities. If an issue arises in the class or as a result of behavior at lunch or breaks, stop the class and call a powwow then and there to troubleshoot. This immediacy often works very well, not only in terms of focusing attention on the problem solving or conflict resolution process, but also on disrupting the trouble causing behavior.

- *Allow for private communication, but resolve the problem as a group.* If an issue is between two students or two factions in the class, it is often necessary to talk privately with one or more of the children to get a clear picture of what is happening and to ensure all sides of the story are fully heard, but then return to the group forum to come to a decision. This encourages the children to see their peers as resources for resolution.

- *Rely on consensus, not majority rule.* Majority rulings are generally divisive because they force people to take sides. Where possible, allow children to work together until they come up with a solution on which everyone more or less agrees. This helps children understand the very crucial skill of compromise. It also emphasizes the value of group harmony. Consensus can be time consuming in the beginning, largely because children are not used to the concept as a formal means of resolution, but they get faster at it with practice. If time is a real issue when problem solving, set a predetermined amount of time at the start. If there is a holdout or two at the end of the time, then *you* make the decision.

- *Regularly express your faith in the group as a capable problem solving body.* Use positive language to encourage the class, such as "I know you can do this," "I know you will come up with a solution that works," or "I trust you to do this well." When a problem is resolved, again comment positively: "You did that well" or "You looked at all the sides and came up with a really good idea" or "You can really figure things out when you get all your heads together."

GROUP CELEBRATIONS

A very special way of uniting the group is to celebrate together. Think of christenings, confirmations, bar mitzvahs, weddings, funerals, and graduations. We don't do these things alone, do we? And why not? Because sharing meaningful moments connects us to those who are ours.

These celebrations don't need to be elaborate or time consuming. Sometimes the chaotic nature of the children, especially when they first arrive in the class, means that parties per se are not possible at all, as this is just too much disorder for some of the children to handle. No problem. In that case, scale it right down to a badge or banner or a cupcake. All that is really important is the opportunity for the whole group to be part of a celebratory experience.

There are several opportunities for celebrations during the school year, some that focus on individuals within the group and others that focus on the group as a whole.

Holidays

This is an obvious source of group celebration, so it is worth mentioning, but in our experience, holidays are too much of a minefield in a culturally mixed class. Even nonreligious holidays like Halloween can be problematic if the class includes children who are, for example, Jehovah's Witnesses. It's not a good group bonding experience if even one child is left out. In schools with a more homogeneous population, such as church schools, or where a given holiday is routinely celebrated schoolwide, here is a good opportunity for the group to enjoy planning and preparing together as well as enjoying the celebration.

Birthdays

Have the rest of the group contribute to planning and preparing for an individual child's birthday. This can take the form of decorating his or her chair, blowing up balloons, and making cards. Let children talk about their own previous experiences with birthday celebrations, as this helps them anticipate what the birthday child will feel.

Accomplishment of Goals

Celebrating individual children's accomplishments is only effective if all the children will eventually have a chance at this kind of attention, and this usually proves to be just a bit too much celebrating for most classrooms. However, celebrating the reaching of a group goal is a very good way of encouraging positive group behavior. Again, this doesn't have to be elaborate. A candy bar each and 10 minutes to sit and chat while eating it works well enough.

Spontaneous Celebrations

Every once in a while it is lovely to just throw out all of the plans and do something fun. These usually happen when the kids have been unusually cooperative, there isn't anything horrible looming in the schedule, and Teacher is in a really good mood. And that's fine. The children are meant to celebrate just the group being the group. And it's important to articulate this. State clearly that this spontaneous celebration is happening just because we, as a group, are special.

10

The Future

Programs for emotional and behavioral disorders are the most problematic and least successful services of special education. Research is consistent regarding the lack of improvement for children enrolled in these programs (Anderson, Kutash, & Duchnowski, 2001; Lane, Barton-Arwood, Nelson, & Wehby, 2008; Maggin, Wehby, Moore-Partin, Robertson, & Oliver, 2011; Siperstein, Wiley, & Forness, 2011).

Follow-up studies show that the educational, behavioral, and social outcomes of children placed in programs for emotional and behavioral disorders are the worst of any special education group. They are isolated, extremely deficient in academic skills, and unprepared socially for the critical transition to work. They do the poorest of any students in percentage in finishing school, finding postschool employment, and in the quality of their young adult lives (U.S. Department of Education, 2006). With such a discouraging set of outcomes, it should come as no surprise that teachers of classrooms for the behaviorally disordered have the highest attrition rate in the field of special education (Bradley, Henderson, & Monfore, 2004).

The dimensions of a relationship-driven classroom model we have talked about in the previous chapters provide a background for a discussion of what constitutes the best practice for children in classrooms for emotional and behavioral disorders. In a relationship-driven approach, a teacher thinks and behaves in substantially different ways than what we would expect from teachers in classes for the behaviorally disordered—given current practice with its emphasis on control. What can be gleaned when the relationship-driven classroom model is juxtaposed to current practice, and what are the implications of such a comparison for best practice?

EMPHASIZE RELATIONSHIPS

The main implication of the relationship-driven classroom model is that relationships should be the central focus in teaching children with emotional and behavioral disorders. Relationships *are* the intervention.

Many if not all children in a classroom for the behaviorally disordered will be hard to reach and resistant. Here are key suggestions for building relationships. Some of them have been addressed earlier, but we are going to reiterate.

Acceptance

Before you can build a relationship with a resistant child, you need to start by accepting him. You need to recognize exactly where someone is when you start to deal with him. And understand the basic principle, actually a principle of physics, that no one or no thing can be at two places at once. That means the child can't be where he is and at the same time be where you think he should be. It's your functional goal to recognize where the child is. Staying in the present and staying with the process helps you do this.

People who focus on goals tend to be judgmental because they are judging people against the final product. If you haven't reached your goal, you are seen as wanting. And that is simply because that's where the focus is. This is like the kid who gets 90% on his paper, and his parents say, "Why didn't you get 100%?" They want to see their kid as perfect, rather than as their kid actually is.

Acceptance is the ground work of trust. And trust, as we learned earlier, is the cornerstone of change. Acceptance is also a crucial aspect of relationship forming. We tend to only form relationships with the people we feel accept us just as we are. Thus, you want to communicate to the child that who he is right now is sufficient for you to want to form a relationship with him. He is okay just as he is. This is necessary in order for the child to find it worth taking a risk to change.

One thing that should be happening all along is to be unequivocally on the child's side. This doesn't mean accepting everything the child does, but making it clear that the child herself is acceptable. The difference between the child and her actions is another way of saying it. You do this by focusing on the child, showing an interest in the child, being present, paying attention, listening to her, and by making it apparent that you care enough about her to correct her behavior. The child needs to know that you care that she isn't likeable and that you want to see that change.

Another way to show acceptance is to be informed about the child's world. We are not only talking about his ethnic and socioeconomic culture but also his generational culture and all of those more superficial things that keep us apart. And finally, use appropriate vocabulary. What this means is don't talk down to him, don't patronize him, and don't try to talk his talk. Ultimately speak to him as an equal because at the end of the day he is equal to you in terms of human dignity and respect.

Commitment

In forming or trying to form relationships with resistant students, the next necessary step after acceptance is to communicate commitment to the children. What is often missing entirely in the lives of difficult children are adults who are willing to commit to them. The etiological condition most often mentioned in the histories of problem children is the lack of adult commitment and care (Perry & Szalavitz, 2006).

Adults show a lack of commitment to children by not spending focused time with them or by not participating with the children when they are spending time with them. They show it by not preferencing the children's needs, by passing them on to other adults so they have multiple caretakers, and by giving up emotionally when the children do not conform to preconceived ideas.

You show commitment to the child by sticking to the process basically. Resistant children are hard to work with, and if you commit to them, you stick to them through thick and thin. When you say "Okay, this is hard; we are not having a good time at that, but I am going to be here for you" it's telling the child that you're going to be there and that you want to be in their presence. You show commitment by showing the willingness to try alternatives.

Seeing From the Other Point of View

Another way of dealing with hard to reach children in encouraging relationships is to have the ability to see from the other point of view. Repeating this point should alert you to how important it is to the relationship model. You need to be able to communicate to the child that you are able to see her point of view.

This is not the same as empathy. Empathy means that you feel somebody else's experiences and pain as if they were your own. What we are looking for is "Yes, I can see your point of view, I can see how you feel that way, and I can see how that could make you act like that, but I am still functional and in control of my emotions, and hence, I am able to show you a better way."

It is important to be objective in expressing your understanding of the child's point of view. Objectivity gives you the ability to leave behind your own feelings, your own judgments, and your perspective to express from his perspective. You use phrases like "that must feel like . . ." or "that must seem to you like . . ." or "if I was in that situation, I would feel like . . ." rather than "I understand." To say "I understand what you are going through" is an enormous assumption on your part. You think you understand, but there's no way to tell whether you really do or not.

Affection

An essential element that helps in forming a relationship with resistant children is the ability to feel genuine affection for the child. Realistic affection and indeed an understanding of what realistic affection means are very important. It doesn't mean you like the child all the time. It's not unconditional love. People who claim to feel unconditional anything are not in touch with the inevitable irritations and frustrations of human relationships. Human relationships are difficult things. We all feel irritations and frustration with the people we love. What we are aiming for is for the child to see you as someone who unambiguously likes her most of the time and that when she does something negative or alienating, you will not break off the relationship. Instead you will use the incident to help her learn to behave more appropriately. That is quite different from unconditional love.

Enthusiasm

Another thing we find really helpful with resistant children is what we are going to call enthusiasm. It is your primary way of communicating your willingness to be with that kid and that you want to form a relationship with him. This should go without saying, but we find it is always helpful to say it anyway, that to do this job you must really like children, and you must like people in general. You are working on a very human level, so if you don't like kids, get out now. If you have the least reservation about being able to interact with children, stop now.

It is also very helpful under this category of enthusiasm for you to have a good memory of your own childhood. It is helpful if you remember how you yourself felt as a child at any given age. This helps you appreciate the child's situation and the child's perspective. So if you can remember back to the inaccuracies that you had as a child, the misperceptions you had as a child, and the hopes you had as a child, your own memories will help guide you in terms of responding to the children you are working with today.

It is also helpful to have childlike personality characteristics. Suffice it to say, there's a big difference between having childlike characteristics and being dysfunctional or childish. So keep that in mind; we are not advising you to act childish. We are not advocating Peter Pan either, because to our minds an adult who hasn't grown up is a dysfunctional adult. What we are looking for in terms of childlike personality characteristics is that you're quick to laugh, that you can see the funny side of things, that you can laugh very genuinely and at yourself, and that you can join in doing silly things.

And the last quality we would list as a childlike personality trait is what we call the *wow* or *gee-whiz* factor. This entails a sense of wonder on your part. Be amazed by the things you see because the world is full of amazing things. Try and maintain this childlike quality because it hard to resist an enthusiastic person.

Boundaries

Next in forming a relationship with a resistant child is your ability to set and communicate boundaries. We have already discussed extensively the setting of boundaries, but how do you communicate this other than the action itself? Obviously, you are setting boundaries when you say to somebody, "Stop." But how else can you communicate it, particularly to somebody who is going to react negatively whenever you tell them to stop? One way is showing that you are in control of yourself; that is, you are able to set limits successfully and consistently on your own behavior. It is also by showing that you're able to stop yourself when you are upset. Many children are difficult or hard to reach because they come from an exceptionally dysfunctional environment where adults cannot stop themselves. These adults cannot set boundaries over their own behavior, whether it is sexual behavior, anger, or some other dysfunctional behavior. Modeling for children is a very useful way of setting boundaries.

Fairness

Another factor in reaching the difficult child is the ability to be fair and impartial. This means you are going to always side with the forces of good, no matter who shows them. If a difficult child shows them against the authority of your school, it's your responsibility to be impartial and stand up for the child. An example that comes to mind was *One Child's* Sheila and her encounter with the principal. Torey was not able to stop her from being corporally punished. But in the aftermath, Torey did her best to make it clear to Sheila that she was willing to understand her side and to take her side and that she felt that the behavior on the part of the principal was wrong.

Being fair and impartial means you provide information and advice to all sides in a conflict. You don't take sides with one against the other. Being fair and impartial means you listen receptively and are interested in both sides of the disagreement. Impartial is another word for being objective.

Teaching

A major qualification in reaching the resistant child is to *always remember you are a teacher.* A teacher's job is to teach. Do not assume therefore that the child knows how to behave. Tackle misbehavior from the perspective of a teacher. That means you need to teach appropriate behavior. Don't approach misbehavior from the perspective that it needs to be punished. That's the curriculum of control. Don't approach it from the perspective that he needs to learn how to obey, and don't approach it from the perspective that his misbehavior is evidence that he is evil or bad.

Break down functional behavior into its components, and teach those components as building blocks. Do not expect the child to master the behavior all at once. We discussed approximation earlier. If you handed a child a violin, would she play you Mozart? No, and it wouldn't be fair for you to expect the child to play Mozart because she has not played the violin before. So it isn't fair to treat kids that way. Teach the components of what you are looking for, and take into account the child's need to approximate behavior.

One-on-One Time

Another method for reaching the resistant child is to spend some one-on-one time with the child each day, even if it's in a group. All relationships require one-on-one time when both parties do not have to vie for the attention of others. It doesn't mean you have to seclude yourself away with the kid, it simply means setting up a situation where everybody else can be screened out, even if they are right there next to you. It might be working in a carrel or it might be working at a table where everybody else is elsewhere. Always try to get one-on-one time each day. It allows for stronger focus and more detailed teaching opportunities. Some things need to be taught to one child at a time, or only to one child in your class. One-on-one allows you to do this. It also shows commitment and willingness on your part for a relationship.

Flexibility

In developing relationships with resistant children, flexibility is an important factor. A certain amount of flexibility is a character trait we think people possess innately. Some of us have more flexible personalities than others or the ability to think on our feet. However, a large part of flexibility is also simple, acquired knowledge. And what that means is you've got a significant amount of behaviors at your fingertips.

This is another way of saying be prepared. If you are prepared, you know several different things you can do in a situation; then you have got flexibility. Flexibility with resistant children in this context means you are capable of using many techniques. If one does not work, you switch to the other. And flexibility also means having the capacity to recognize when something needs to be adapted because if you leave it as it is, kids are going to have meltdowns, or the situation is going to get boring or out of control, and produce bad behavior. So it's not only knowing what to change to; it's also the ability to recognize that you need to change.

Modeling

Another aspect of working with hard to reach students is the ability to use modeling and identification effectively. We said earlier how important modeling is. If you develop a positive relationship with a child, the child will begin to identify with you. You want this. You are a functional adult, and you want him to identify with you. It's normal that he should do so. This is basically how children learn to be adults.

While using modeling and identification with hard to reach children, it's extremely important for you to remember at all times that you are the adult. So, as a consequence, you always need to be able to keep all this identification healthy and within boundaries. This means that while the child may become very dependent on you, you don't become too personal. It's also important to watch out for those times where identification becomes so strong that the children are no longer being true to themselves. They so want to be like you that they are no longer giving credence to their own identity. When that happens, it is time to remain loving and supportive but to point out that you have differences, that it's all right to have differences, and it doesn't affect the relationship.

The other factor in using modeling and identification with these children is to continually try to model appropriate behavior yourself. Or you can present other respected figures that the child would like to emulate as examples of appropriate behavior. The example that Torey used in *Beautiful Child* was the comic superhero, She-Ra, Princess of Power. She-Ra had character traits that Venus very much wanted super powers that Torey personally did not have. But here was a character that had them and allowing Venus to model herself on that and identify with the character allowed her to integrate those characteristics with herself.

Behavioral Change

In dealing with students who are hard to reach, the ability to *teach them how to change behavior is vital*. Teach is the important word here. There is no other way of going about it. As we have mentioned before, teach the children how thinking precedes emotion, even when we are not aware of it. Show them, and get them to step back so they can see what thought they are having before they feel and before they act. Teach that we need to change our thinking first before we can change our feelings and our actions.

If you have a child who is making racist remarks, you can either punish him, and then he just complies out of obedience, or you can teach him what kind of thoughts he's having first that give him the feelings that make him want to make those remarks. When you do that, when you change his thinking, you'll automatically change his feelings. Consider the child who has never had the opportunity to interact with someone else of another race or another culture, and he has heard at home that Muslims are bad and dangerous. Muslims are evil, of course; they blew up the Twin Towers. So that's the thinking. We treat them badly because we think they blew up the Twin Towers. The opportunity to meet a Muslim child and discover the child is just like him allows him to change his feelings toward the child, and that ultimately allows the result of stopping the racist remarks.

Many difficult behaviors are found in a child's belief system. John Locke, the English philosopher, in 1690 wrote that "No person's knowledge can go past his experience." None of us can know about things of which we have no experience. So, as a consequence, if a child only knows of herself as inept, as bad, as guilty, or only knows of herself as somebody who's abused or used, she's not going to be able to overcome her past. She cannot be a different person because she does not have any experience of being a different person. It is important to work on changing thinking so that you can change the feelings and eventually the behavior.

Recognize Power Struggles and Disengage From Them

It's important not to feel personally threatened by directed, inappropriate behavior. Don't take things personally. Most of life is not personal. This gets back to the issue of subjectivity versus objectivity. If you are a subjective thinker you tend to think the whole world is about you, and therefore everything is directed at you, and you have caused it all to happen, and it's your fault. The truth is you are not that important so you might as well look objectively at it. Chances are that the reacting child doesn't feel personally about you at all; you just happened to be in the way. So don't feel personally threatened by misbehavior. And don't feel the need to triumph, or show who is boss. Most of the kids are really super at power struggles. They are probably already better at them than you are. The really important thing to remember here is you are the boss. You have already achieved that status. You don't need to prove it, and if you are proving it, all you are really playing is one-upmanship. That is not functional, and it is usually completely ineffective. Know how to pick your battles. There are sometimes when you are going to have to stand firm because it is an important issue. The child must comply. So if you are going to have a power struggle in which you win, make sure it is over something that must be fought.

Have alternatives ready for disengagement. One of the best is planned ignoring. Tomaso in *Somebody Else's Kids* was a legend in his own time in terms of power struggles. He had developed Driving-Teacher-Nuts tactics to a high art. One of his most effective weapons was his ability to pass wind. He could do it any time he chose and at any decibel level. Up on one buttock he would rise and aim so that his victim received full benefit of the smell and sound. "It must have been the beans I ate," he would always say sweetly. The crowning touch involved pulling his pants out in back and sticking a hand down to feel. God only knows what he was checking; Torey never asked. For that kind of behavior, inattention seemed the soundest recourse. It took weeks, but the Driving-Teacher-Nuts behaviors eventually stopped, and Tomaso went from strength to strength after that point.

Another method that is useful in disengaging is to actively agree with the child. If the child picks an argument with you, or calls you a name, or says you are being unfair, just say "Yes, I am, aren't I." It's almost impossible to argue with you if you agree and if you keep agreeing. Again, classroom crises are actually opportunities to teach. See if you can turn it into a teaching opportunity instead of a power struggle.

Realistic Expectations

With kids change happens slowly. Show genuine regard for their ability to change, but be realistic. In terms of tackling problems do realize that the difficult or resistant child, or probably every other single child in your class, does not come to you wanting to change. Take this as a given. They are not coming with open arms saying, "Hey, wonderful teacher, do this for me." As a consequence, we have found that it helps to go in with an attitude of seduction.

You are going to have to charm them into wanting to change. Think of charming ways. Joy begets joy. Enjoy what you are doing. Be excited about your class. That is seductive. Stories, read-alouds, those are seductive. Most kids can't resist joining things like that. Creative writing, art, and musical activities are also often very seductive. Kids like to express themselves. Drama and puppets are seductive. Most kids enjoy these types of activities. Cooking was a favorite in Torey's class. Very few people do not like to eat, and very few people do not like to make a mess. Cooking is wonderful because it combines both of those. Field trips, and we are not talking about going to the White House, even a field trip to the other side of the playground will do quite good enough. A field trip to look at the dirt in the playground will do it sometimes. Nature observation itself is seductive. We don't know what happens to adults, but we have yet to meet a kid who doesn't like nature.

Somewhere along the way we lose it, but even the most resistant kids can usually be seduced into enjoying something in the natural world. And in the same way, this is true for science activities. Again, though somewhere along the way we may lose kids' interest as they get older, and we don't know why, most kids we know love building a volcano, love reading about dinosaurs, love rock collecting, and things of this sort. Science activities tend to be very seductive and to be things that even the most hard-to-reach child wants to take part in.

RETHINK BEHAVIOR MODIFICATION

A relationship-driven classroom offers an alternative to classrooms of control. By focusing on relationships there is better access to the internal, unobservable world of the child—her thoughts, fears, actions, and reactions. Getting to know the child then allows the teacher to choose which methods and techniques are best suited for the job of working with that individual child. This approach is opposed to the ubiquitous one-size-fits-all approach which starts out with a strict behavior modification approach applied to everyone. A relationship-driven approach allows the teacher to wait and see what he is dealing with before making choices. Starting with a behavior modification system places the emphasis on control rather than on the relationship with the teacher. Children learn to relate to the behavior modification system and not the authority figure, and behavior gains do not transfer well to the mainstream classroom where things are not so tightly controlled. It becomes almost impossible for the child to respond reliably to the teacher in a setting which does not include some kind of behavior modification. Thus, while one may have immediate results from starting with behavior modification, it seldom transfers well out of a setting and is instead simply situation specific.

Starting with a relationship also gives the teacher a chance to observe and understand group dynamics, which, of course, are different for each classroom. Most children in classrooms

for behavioral disorders have poor social skills that will under-
mine them in the real world. Starting with a behavior modification program often destroys normal group dynamics. Having
a chance to observe class dynamics naturally gives one an idea
of how to form a cohesive group and develop more appropriate social skills for the specific group within the context of the
natural group dynamics. These are the dynamics that will be
replicated in the real world.

Behavior modification does have a place in the relationship-
driven classroom as a motivator for change. Food, star charts,
sticker charts, class parties and celebrations, and field trips
can be used as rewards and motivators for individual and
group change. Torey had a bag with small toys and other small
rewards in it, and if the child reached a certain goal she could
pick anonymously from there, and the element of surprise or
mystery was sometimes motivating.

What is important to note is that these stars, stickers, field
trips, and so on are substitutes or concrete symbols of relationships. An M&M can get a child to behave appropriately, but it's
a symbol of good behavior, and it's a symbol of a relationship.
Behavior modification symbols cannot replace a relationship. If
you replace a relationship with a concrete consequence on a too
often basis you encourage apathy. Who can relate to an M&M
or a tic or a star? There is nothing there to relate to, so it teaches
apathy. It also teaches disaffection. You are not connected to
something so you don't feel connection. And it also teaches lack
of empathy or an inability to see something from another point
of view. There is no point of view in an M&M. And an M&M
has no feelings, so you're not teaching the child how to perceive
or interpret feelings. And finally it teaches subjectivity and self-
centeredness. Subjectivity is basically selfishness. It is seeing
things from one's own point of view. When a child works for
rewards from you, you are teaching subjectivity. Selfishness
comes quite natural to us, so it is probably something we don't
want to reward on a whole scale effort.

Behavior modification is an effective tool, but a tool is all
it is. Consider the analogy of a hammer. If your classroom is a

house, you would not want to build a house without a hammer. But at the end of the day, you don't want to say, "This is the house the hammer built." The hammer was simply a tool that was used. It is one of many tools that is necessary to build a complete house. It shouldn't be the centerpiece of what you do.

EMPHASIZE ACADEMICS AND INTELLECTUAL PURSUITS

Many, if not most, students in classrooms for behavioral disorders are underachieving, with more than half experiencing learning difficulties or disabilities. Academic deficits tend to persist or worsen for children after being placed in classrooms for the behaviorally disordered (Nelson, Benner, Lane, & Smith, 2004). On average these students perform one to two grade levels behind their peers while in elementary school, and by the time they reach high school are performing three to four grade levels below their peers (Reid, Gonzalez, Nordness, Trout, & Epstein, 2004). The lack of progress experienced by these students raises serious questions about the effectiveness of educational programming used in these classrooms.

Academic success is a focus of a relationship-driven classroom. At the heart of academic success is motivation. When we are motivated to learn, it is much easier to focus, much easier to listen to what the teacher is saying, and much easier to retain it. Well-motivated students are, by default, better-behaved students because they will be spending more time on task. The teacher can encourage motivation in the following ways:

- *Stay in the process yourself as much as possible.* Paying attention to what each child is doing as he is doing it is very important. Students lose motivation when things become too hard or too easy or when they become confused about what they are doing. Being aware and available to them is the most efficient way of moving them past these difficulties before they become stuck and totally lose focus. It has the added advantage of making it clear you care how they are doing and are interested enough to pay attention.

- *Be reasonably prepared.* The relationship-driven method is all about spontaneity, all about staying in the present in order to flexibly respond to student needs as they arise. Too many people, however, mistake *spontaneous* for *unprepared*, and this cannot be further from the truth. People who are spontaneous or flexible are those who have choices at their fingertips. Virtually none of us is so bright or creative as to be able to think up viable alternatives on the spot without previously having considered what possibilities are available to us.

  The main reason people link spontaneity with lack of preparedness is because they link preparedness with the teacher who rigidly sticks to his excruciatingly detailed lesson plan, and we know all too well how demotivating that kind of teaching usually is. That isn't preparedness, because it has nothing to do with how well one knows the material one is teaching or the many ways to go about it. It is, instead, about maintaining control, either personal control or control over an environment that feels unsafe. That's a different issue altogether. What we are looking for is to develop enough structure and planning to make us comfortable with what we are teaching each day, because this confidence will allow both flexibility and enhancement of our own enthusiasm for the material. That will, in turn, motivate the students.

- *Deemphasize comparisons in the relationship-driven classroom.* We talked about comparisons previously and the damage they do to group harmony. They are also serious motivation killers because only a few children are going to routinely meet the competitive criteria for success. In order for all students in the classroom to stay motivated and progress, it is important to put the focus on competing only with themselves and on doing the best they can at the moment. Restructure traditional methods of recognition. Recognition of effort *is* a helpful motivator, but simply going for highest scores results in nothing more than winners, who are very often repeatedly the winners, and losers, who often assume they will never win, so don't try. Focus instead on recognizing those who have most improved or, at the very least, give equal recognition to much improved students as to high scores.

- *Deemphasize grades, and emphasize learning.* School is actually not about getting good grades, even for regular students. It is about learning. In the current social and political climate, it's easy to lose this point. Help children recapture the magic of learning as a real and present activity. Help them understand that there are things all of us are interested in learning, and we're on an adventure to find those things. This approach provides motivation that abstract grades cannot.

- *Be flexible about learning formats.* People really do have different learning styles and this will be even more apparent in a special education classroom where differences make children less adaptable. As teachers, we need to be aware that some children will be visual, some will be auditory, some will need multiple modalities stimulated, some will have low blood sugar, and so on, and these varying factors will affect the child's motivation to learn. While it isn't possible to adapt lessons to take into account every child's individual learning style, nor should we try, it is still important to be aware of the differences and the impact they may have and to be flexible when necessary. Personalize learning when possible. At the very least, vary the lessons to focus on different modalities over the course of the day.

- *Never underestimate the value of unexpected learning situations.* Teach less to what you've planned and more to what you've got. Motivation is process oriented. We can only be motivated now. Thus, what is happening now usually makes an excellent lesson because it already has our attention. If a butterfly comes through the window, watch it. See how it flies. Does it flap its wings up and down or back and forth? Does it flap all the time or does it glide? Catch it. Look at it under a magnifying glass. Let it go outside and watch where it goes. How high does it fly? Why? What would you do if you were a butterfly? How would you feel if some giant came along and caught you? In the same way, if the class has a meltdown, teach problem solving. Why did that happen? What built up to it? How can we do it differently next time?

- *Use variety of presentation.* Make use of the wide diversity of learning materials and methods available—seatwork, rote learning, visualizations, audiovisuals, group work, individual work, and so on. Our brains use a special area for tasks we are newly learning, and when we are working from that place, we are present oriented and paying attention. As soon as we become familiar with a task, it is moved to a whole different part of the brain where we store known material. This is our automatic area and we can often do these familiar things without being present at all. Think about driving and how very often our mind wanders so far away from what we are doing that we drive past our exit or we arrive someplace without remembering having driven by familiar landmarks. Obviously we miss a lot of what is happening around us when we go into automatic pilot, and things can happen that we don't want or we miss opportunities for things that we do want. Familiarity is what allows us to switch from the attention-paying place in our brain to the known place when we turn on automatic pilot. This can happen either through familiarity with the task itself or through familiarity with the setting. So strive for enough familiarity in your daily routine to provide a sense of safety, so the children feel confident of what to expect, but use enough variety to keep them oriented in the present. Motivation is gone the moment our minds wander off into daydreams or plans or what happened last week.

- *Provide successful experiences.* Provide students with realistic challenges with a high ratio of success to failure. Competence is crucial, and the best therapy for children is to learn skills and competencies. Self-esteem isn't passive. It's active, and it comes from mastering your world, from being competent, and from being in control. For any student, especially those who do not expect it, success is exhilarating, motivating, and joyful. Nicholas Hobbs, past president of the American Psychological Association, states, "It is like spitting from the top of a windmill" (as cited in Valore, 2007, p. 212).

- *Focus on students' strengths and interests instead of their deficiencies.* Teaching to children's strengths and interests helps them explore and develop their potentials and capabilities. New knowledge is built using children's previous knowledge, experiences, and skills. This encourages students to initiate activities of interest to them.

  For example, in *Just Another Kid*, the one area in which Shamie, a refugee from battle-torn Northern Ireland, excels is European history. He is fascinated by the past, and history is the only area in which he can be enticed into doing extra reading. Shamie is put on a course of studying medieval Europe and efforts are made to coordinate as many other activities to the subject as possible. These included tied-in math projects, spelling lists, art activities, preparing a medieval meal, and building a model castle to scale.

  Likewise, when *Beautiful Child's* Billy shows a fascination with a coffee table book about tulips, Torey brings in her old botany textbooks from college. She teaches him how to dissect flowers and draw the parts, and he keeps a notebook and draws pictures and diagrams of what he has seen. Billy works meticulously identifying stamens, pollens, and more, and in the process improves his organization and study skills.

  And in *Somebody Else's Kids*, 12-year-old Claudia, burdened by pregnancy and depression, is given a great deal of latitude in choosing the academic projects she pursues. Enrichment activities are designed, Claudia's knowledge in weak areas is broadened, and she is allowed to choose research fields in which she is personally interested. She would later graduate valedictorian of her high school class.

ACTIVELY TEACH SOCIAL-EMOTIONAL SKILLS

Widely accepted social skills training packages used with students who have emotional and behavioral disorders follow a skill deficit approach. Social skills deficits are clearly delineated, scope and sequence are outlined, and teaching approaches are scripted. There is little need for adjustment, dialogue, or conversational learning.

A review of 13 reviews examining social skills training packages for students with emotional and behavioral disorders found them to be of limited effectiveness and lacking generalization (Maag, 2006). The general consensus is that formal social skills training programs have not produced behavioral changes that make students with emotional and behavioral disorders more socially acceptable (Kauffman & Landrum, 2009).

We do not think one can teach social-emotional skills in the abstract. Scripted social skill lesson plans take socialization out of context, when socialization by definition is highly contextualized learning. In the relationship-driven classroom social-emotional skills being taught are integrated into real situations that occur in the classroom rather than teaching them separately from the academic curriculum and the classroom management system.

One actively teaches social-emotional skills like one teaches math or science. Do not assume that simply modeling these skills for students or providing a 4- to 6-week unit on social skills is sufficient for learning. Actively and regularly teach social-emotional skills in the context of classroom life. Teaching social-emotional skills is an ongoing process. This isn't something you teach in a unit and say, "Okay, this is done; you've got it."

In the relationship-driven classroom, children live and work in groups. Only in group context will their social-emotional strengths and weaknesses be revealed, thus giving the teacher the material for teaching and learning. These notions about what is pedagogically necessary to teach social-emotional skills to children runs counter to conventional wisdom in special education. Common wisdom exhorts teachers to separate children from each other for doing their academic work. In many classrooms for the behaviorally disordered, it is quite common to have the children working separately at desks or carrels in order to avoid bringing the students together for group style lessons.

A variety of programs exist to help teachers incorporate social-emotional skills into the daily curriculum. The Collaborative for Academic, Social, and Emotional Learning (CASEL), an organization based at the University of Illinois in Chicago, has helped school systems around the world bring these programs into their curriculum. CASEL advocates for instructional practices that used repeated rehearsal of social-emotional skills and prompting and cueing the use of those skills throughout the school day in natural contexts. CASEL recommends that social-emotional learning be infused into the entire curriculum and not simply a fragmented add-on (Zins, Elias, Weissberg, et al., 1998).

INCLUDE EXPRESSIVE AND CREATIVE ARTS

The focus on education in today's school systems is clearly directed toward the requirements of the No Child Left Behind Act of 2001, aiming to ensure all children are academically proficient by 2014. This act has changed the face of education and has taken the traditional environment that encourages holistic learning through reading, writing, arithmetic, and the arts and transformed it into a rigid structure based on test scores (Vigilone, 2009).

Authentic education, however, blends both cognitive and affective goals (Morse, 2008). Counter to common practice in programs for emotional and behavioral disorders, a relationship-driven classroom has a substantial segment devoted to the expressive arts. Writing, art, music, movement experiences, and drama are natural ways for children to externalize and deal with feelings.

Expressive writing is part of the curriculum in a relationship-driven classroom. Dialogue or interactive journals are spiral bound notebooks in which children can record daily what they feel; their ups and downs; their hopes, wishes, and dreams; things that happened to them; and other important events in their lives. Children are free to express their opinions on anything—even a negative opinion of the teacher and her teaching methods—without fear of retaliation. Each evening the teacher goes through the entries and leaves notes or comments to the children about what they had written. It is a personal communication, and this allows the teacher and the children to find out how the other feels. Research shows that children in classrooms for emotional and behavioral disorders view dialogue journals as useful forums for increasing self-awareness and discussing issues (Regan, 2003).

It is also through art activities that one can gain insight into children's thoughts and emotions. Sigmund Freud in his early studies of psychoanalysis discovered that artwork done by disturbed patients could communicate patients' emotions and events that language could not. Freud found that images were less anxiety-provoking forms of communication. Steele (2009) has documented that drawing activities provide a safe vehicle to communicate what children often have few words to describe.

Musical activities also play an important role. In *Beautiful Child*, singing took place every day to bond the group. Songs that were funny, could be mimed, and stood up well to being sung with gusto were favorites. Singing was used to calm the children, to lift their spirits, distract the group's attention away from doing things they shouldn't, and as a good way to transition the children from one activity to another. Singing was also used as a form of contingent reinforcement, the group singing every time someone made it through a whole period with his or her traffic light on green.

Mike had a fantastic student in his graduate classes years back, and the student was a teacher in an elementary class for behavior disorders. He had formed an Appalachian dulcimer band with his class, and they traveled around in a small school bus putting on concerts for retirement homes and the like. The class wasn't a cohesive group until they started the band and musical activity. It was all basic stuff—no Mozart or anything—but it was like one of those demonstrations of magnetism you see where the iron filings are flopped down every which way until you pass a magnet over them and they snap into alignment. The kids in his class could be any which way, in all kinds of moods, and when music was involved they snapped into a cohesive group.

A relationship-driven classroom allows for mobility. Children need mobility. You need to move around in the environment to feel safe in all parts of the environment. Torey incorporated movement experiences through the daily schedule beginning with morning discussion, during subject transition times, and during content lessons. Ann Green Gilbert's *Teaching the Three Rs Through Movement Experiences* (1977) provides hundreds of examples of creative movement experiences targeted to lessons in language arts, math, social studies, science, and the arts. There is ample evidence that movement activity throughout the day can help all students with their concentration and attention and reduce disruptive behavior (Mulrine, Prater, & Jenkins, 2008).

Hobbs (1994), who pioneered ecological models for emotionally disturbed children, put forth the principle that each child should know some joy each day and look forward to some joyous event for the morrow. The arts can be employed to program joyous and happy experiences for the children. The arts connect children to one another and make them part of a community for the length of the activity. This may be extremely important for children who either feel they are separated from the group or who feel they do not have the social skills to be a part of a community or a group.

SUPPORT A CONTINUUM
OF ALTERNATIVE PLACEMENTS

The Individuals with Disabilities Education Improvement Act of 2004 mandates that all school-age handicapped children are eligible for a free and appropriate public school education in the least restrictive environment. Currently some educators believe the least restrictive environment is the general education classroom. Proponents of this view advocate full inclusion of all children in general education classrooms (Sapon-Shevin, 2007). Others believe that least restrictive means movement from one placement to another, especially in the direction of the general education classroom (Kauffman & Hallahan, 2005).

We agree there is a place for integrating regular and special education. The problem is it needs to be very individualized and go child by child to provide a suitable match. No single reintegration plan can be suggested for all children, because each student's return to the regular classroom is associated with a number of variables.

Structure and routine are very important when considering educational placement.

Our long experience in this area convinces us that *all* children need structure and most thrive best on routine. Routine is a much undervalued factor, and we are patiently waiting for some new study to come along and tell us this as news, so that we can go back to providing routine without feeling retro. This does not mean that we should return to a time when all classes were self-contained, because a well-organized teacher and school can provide plenty of both structure and routine in the open-plan systems. Some children, however, will always need more structure largely because, for whatever reason, they do not have it internally. These children will always cope better in a self-contained room. Thus, this should remain an educational option.

A continuum of placements is essential. To appropriately prepare a child for success in school sometimes requires specialized interventions that are unfeasible in the regular classroom (Zigmond & Kloo, 2011). We believe we should think in terms of the most enabling environment rather than the least restrictive. Treating children equally does not mean treating them the same.

What we need to address here is how to give special education children the education they need without discriminating against them. This leads into the much larger, very pertinent question of prejudice and bigotry, in general, which is really at the base of this whole issue. The question is not why can't the regular classroom teacher meet the needs of this special education child? The real question is how can we treat this individual in a manner that is of equal quality to that of others, regardless of handicap, IQ, socioeconomic background, race, religion, nationality, gender, or other factors? And the answer lies in all of us, not just the classroom teacher.

RETHINK MEDICATION OF STUDENTS

In the 1990s, prescriptions for psychiatric drugs to children and adolescents skyrocketed in the United States (Foltz, 2012). Seventy-five percent of the world's stimulant medication is now prescribed to the children in the United States—more than four times the rest of the world combined (International Narcotics Control Board, 2007). It is estimated that as many as five million children are taking some form of psychiatric medication with stimulants ranking as most popular and antidepressants second (APA Working Group on Psychoactive Medications for Children and Adolescents, 2006). Given indisputable trends, widespread marketing, and growing acceptance of medical intervention, current prevalence is likely greater.

Parents of students with emotional and behavioral disorders report that about half take medication for their disability (Special Education Elementary Longitudinal Study [SEELS], 2003). Stimulants, antidepressants, and antianxiety drugs are the most commonly prescribed medications. SEELS research also points to an increasingly commonplace trend, polypharmacy: the prescribing of two or more medications simultaneously. A survey of psychiatric medications for children with emotional disturbance placed in residential treatment facilities found an overall medication rate of 76% (Ryan, Reid, Gallagher, & Ellis, 2008). Clearly children with emotional and behavioral disorders are the most heavily medicated population in special education.

Critics charge that scientific grounding for widespread psychiatric drugging of children is, at best, unconvincing. Stimulant medication is most commonly used in the treatment of behaviors associated with attention-deficit/hyperactivity disorder. Despite being prescribed to millions of youth, there are no short- or long-term studies demonstrating that academic achievement improves with the use of these stimulants (APA Working Group on Psychoactive Medications for Children and Adolescents, 2006), and there are well publicized medical risks associated with their use (Poulton, 2005). Breggin (2000) contends the public schools use stimulants to control behavioral problems that could be adequately controlled by modifications in the environment, such as changing adults' interactions with the child.

The effectiveness of antidepressants in children is also highly questionable (Kirsch 2010), while there are considerable scientific data on their adverse side effects (Breggin, 2008). Antidepressants now carry a black box warning for suicidal behavior in children and youth and also a lengthy warning section about abnormal behavioral reactions. In addition, antidepressants and anticonvulsant medications used in the treatment of bipolar disorder, and antipsychotic medications designed to treat such conditions as schizophrenia, all interfere with chemicals in the brain involved in social bonding, attachment, and trust building. Under these medication conditions, some youth may be at a disadvantage for establishing a trusting connection. Rather than seeing a detached style from the child as resistance, teachers should be mindful that it may also be a reflection of medication intervention (Foltz, 2008).

We too have extremely strong feelings against the widespread use of drug therapy with children with emotional disorders. Yes, there are some children who definitely benefit from drug therapy, but our experience is also that they are a very small minority. At the height of Torey's teaching, she insisted, relatively successfully, that all of her children be off medication for behavior for at least the first six weeks in her class. This was easier to do in the 1970s and early 1980s, as drugs were only just starting to be used in this way, so normally only a few children were medicated. When doing this, it was relatively easy for Torey to discern those kids who had a genuine problem that profited from drug intervention, and there were a few. She doubts, however, there were more than 10 kids over the course of her career whom she felt needed regular medication for behavioral problems. All the rest responded just fine to a structured classroom and consistent routine.

The initial question then is why has there been this huge explosion in drug prescription for American children? Why do they now need to be medicated? Our suspicion—and this is simply our opinion and nothing more—is that medication is the most expedient way. It is a faster method of getting results than the old-fashioned interaction way, and in this era of instant results and overbusy lives, this makes it the intervention of choice. Moreover, it targets the child and does not require change on the part of anyone else involved. This is more convenient for the adults who may not want to make the lifestyle changes involved to produce the necessary changes in child behavior.

Teachers are obligated to not take the easy road and abandon teaching and interaction skills in favor of a quick fix. One should not discount the abilities of children to develop solutions to even the most daunting dilemmas given support and encouragement. The belief that change will and does occur naturally and universally is the foundation of a relationship-driven methodology.

USE TEACHER NARRATIVE IN TEACHER EDUCATION

The most frequent criticism of Torey's books in relation to classroom methodology is that they are stories, not precise historical accounts of her time in the classroom. The implication is that this lack of literalism makes them not true and that in turn renders the methodology in them also not true because the classroom portrayed in the narrative did not exist literally as described.

In the preface, Torey addressed the reasons why she chose to write the books as narratives. However, it is also important to address why one would choose to use stories at all to convey something as concrete and rational as methodology. Indeed, since the dawn of the scientific area, emphasis has shifted to logic and empiricism as the appropriate path to *real* or *legitimate* truth, and as a consequence, concerted efforts have been made to eliminate the role of the story in our professional lives.

Over the last few decades, a growing number of scholars have looked at the role of narrative—stories—as a fundamental component of human cognition every bit as important to our ability to understand, explain, and communicate human experience as logic and reason.

Perhaps most prominent among these scholars has been psychologist and educator Jerome Bruner, who has devoted much of his academic career to examining the importance of stories in our lives. In his book *Making Stories: Law, Literature, and Life* (2002), he argues that we are hardwired to respond to stories. Our brains intuitively understand the story format. His research indicated the following:

- Humans are innately motivated by stories and pay attention to material presented in story form.
- Humans are innately hardwired to create stories to understand the world around them.
- Humans innately understand new material more easily when it is presented in story form.
- Humans retain information longer that has been presented in story form.
- Humans innately identify characters in stories as symbolic models.

Bradford Mott and others (Mott, McQuiggan, Lee, Lee, & Lester, 2006) state that narrative can be used as an effective tool for exploring the structure and process of "meaning making" and go on to point out that learning which depends on extrinsic motivation often fails to engage students and goes unused, whereas narrative centered learning can provide the four key intrinsic motivators:

1. Challenge: narrative centered learning can feature problem-solving episodes that are not too easy and not too hard;

2. Curiosity: narrative centered learning can stimulate a desire to know what comes next or to engage with interesting characters;

3. Control: narrative centered learning can empower students to take control of their own learning experiences; and

4. Fantasy: narrative centered learning is inherently fantasy based and can contribute to vivid imaginative experiences.

As Bruner (1985) indicated, there are different ways to learn. In special education teacher education, we may have come to value only one kind of thinking, the linear or the logical. Bruner emphasized two modes of learning: the narrative and intuitive as well as the logical and scientific, each differing radically in how it establishes truth. One verifies by appealing to the formal verification practices of empirical proof, while the other establishes unproven likenesses. The logic/scientific mode collects and refines data leading to the discovery of law like principles, while the narrative/intuitive mode constructs stories and drama leading to insights about the human condition. Teacher education needs to search for a balance between the logic/scientific and the narrative/intuitive. Each approach represents a kind of *knowing* essential to teacher education.

Mike has been using teacher narratives in teacher education since 1992, and his arithmetic tells him some 2,500 teachers have sat at desks in his university classrooms and discussed Torey's stories in an attempt to understand effective practice in special education. Mike and his colleagues in a series of studies (Marlowe, 1999, 2006; Marlowe & Maycock, 2000, 2001; Marlowe, Maycock, Palmer & Morrison, 1997) have analyzed teachers' journal entries about the experience of reading Torey's stories.

Overall, the phenomenological structure of the teachers' experience of reading Torey was one of identification with Torey's character leading to new feelings and new knowledge. Teachers noted admiration for Torey's character and referred to her as a role model, a mentor, and an ego ideal. They reported seeing the world of the classroom through the eyes of Torey's character, of putting themselves in Torey's perspective to experience what Torey was experiencing, and to call on Torey's character as a resource when dealing with their own real-world problems.

Teachers consistently reported a preference for reading Torey's stories over professional texts in teacher education. Her stories were seen as more real and true to life, providing real life examples from which to learn classroom techniques and a template for day-to-day interactions with difficult children. While textbooks were seen as having value, they were also described as dull, encyclopedic, and sanitized.

Mike and Gayle Disney conducted a follow-up survey (Marlowe & Disney, 2007) that examined practicing teachers' perceptions of the long-term influence of reading Torey's stories in preservice teacher education. Survey participants ($N = 132$) had enrolled in Mike's preservice course on the education of emotionally disturbed children over a 10-year period (1992–2001). Torey's books had served as course texts. The participants had an average of 5 years of teaching experience.

Participants rated Torey's stories as highly influential in shaping their ability to form relationships with students. Howard Gardner (2006) suggests there are at least eight intelligences, two of which have a direct bearing on one's capacity to relate to others. One he defines as interpersonal intelligence, the capacity to sense and respond properly to the internal states of others. Participants credited Torey with modeling the ability to take the perspective of another and respond appropriately to the moods and motivations of that other. She was cited as a model for warmth and sensitivity; for talking an out-of-control student down or a depressed student up; for handling anger, anxiety, and sadness; for building trust and being respectful; and for creating a sense of belonging.

The other intelligence having a direct bearing on forming relationships is what Gardner terms intrapersonal intelligence, access and knowledge about one's own feelings to use in guiding one's behavior. Participants reported that reading Torey encouraged them to engage in self-examination; to become self-aware; to know themselves; to know their traits, their temperament, and their experiences; and to understand how these relate to how they act and react to children.

The survey contained four open-ended questions. Regarding Question 1 ("How strong an influence was Hayden compared to other influences, practices, and texts used to prepare you to teach?"), 83% of the respondents indicated Torey was a very strong influence: "Her books opened my eyes to a new world," "reading Torey was the ultimate tool in preparing me to meet the demands of my classroom," and "a tremendous influence. I continue to seek answers through her books."

Regarding Question 2 ("Did reading Hayden permanently change your attitudes and beliefs about students with disabilities? Why or why not?"), 62% of respondents stated Torey had positively changed their attitudes toward children with disabilities: "Absolutely—Torey's philosophy is based on 'yes, you can,' and after learning about her progress with students it makes me eager to live the same philosophy." Another 20% stated that Torey had not changed but rather reaffirmed their existing positive attitudes: "She reaffirmed my belief in humanity as a whole."

Regarding Question 3 ("How did reading Hayden help you to develop your identity as a teacher?"), 95% of the respondents indicated Torey's stories had a positive effect on their teacher identities. The most salient theme was Torey's impact as a role model for personal identification: "She is the model special education teacher, and she gives me something to strive for."

Finally, regarding Question 4 ("What adjectives would you use to describe the qualities you see in yourself that remind you of Hayden?"), *caring* was the teacher identity attribute most linked to Torey's influence, followed by *patient, compassionate, loving,* and *understanding.*

Participants reported rereading Torey to renew the positive feelings the stories engendered, to gain insight into their own lives as teachers, and to help them with a difficult teaching situation ("When I recognize that I am beginning to feel discouraged or ineffective, I pull out a Torey Hayden book and reread it. They always remind me of what I can be").

Stories promote engagement and relationships. Stories challenge educators to consider teaching as an ethical, moral undertaking. Stories present difficult dilemmas, hard decisions, and choices. Nel Noddings (2003) writes about the importance of an "ethic of caring." She contends that commitment to care of others is the cornerstone of a helping profession like teaching. She proposes increasing the use of stories in teacher education because they can increase interest, add cultural literacy, enhance human relations, and connect studies to great existential questions.

Noddings (1991) claims that "stories have the power to direct and change our lives" (p. 157). Research on Torey's stories' and teacher education outcomes support Noddings' position. Teachers who read her stories reported they were changed for the better, and these changes endured over time.

FINAL THOUGHTS ON THE RELATIONSHIP-DRIVEN CLASSROOM

An intensely up close and personal approach tends to be effective with children, and yet it can be very hard if the end of the school year comes before the child is ready. Torey has developed a philosophy of attachment and loss in forming relationships which threads through most of her books, especially

One Child and *The Tiger's Child*. As Sheila illustrates, an up-close and personal style does hurt.

When questioned on her website's message board about caring and the extent of involvement in her students' lives and where one draws lines, Torey responded:

> I find it easy to love people—anyone literally—if this person's care is given to me. I find it easy to get up close and personal and to stay there until I get the job done. I find it easy to care in a very real way. But, and this is an important "but," I also find it naturally easy to be objective at almost all times, to keep my personal needs out of the picture, to keep an eye on the timeframe, to know at all times where the boundaries are. I suppose the best analogy to what is going on here is akin to the comradeship in war—how men tend to form strong bonds during the time they are together under duress of war and matter greatly to each other for that time, but when the war is over, they all part and go their separate ways, often keeping in touch but nothing more. (Hayden, 2001)

Forming relationships is central to teaching, but it inevitably implies eventual loss, just the way birth inevitably contains within it the guarantee of eventual death. A favorite quote is "A ship in the harbor is safe, but that's not what ships were built for." In other words, the only certain way to stay safe from loss is never having attachment, but attachments and forming relationships are an essential part of what it means to be human. We are a social species. We are primed biologically to have relationships from birth. If they are not given to us, we actively seek them out, even in the first minutes of life. In the few known tragic instances where children have been kept isolated and confined away from others and later discovered, while they have a very difficult time indeed adjusting and some have never made the transition successfully, all of them have immediately tried to form relationships. This is for what we are innately designed.

That Torey formed attachments, which she knew ultimately would end, simply meant she was able to keep an objective eye on what was going on in her teacher–student relationships—I'm a teacher; my ending comes in June—not that she was any better at loss than were her students or that it hurt her any less. Part of what she teaches in forming an attachment, is how to cope with loss, and loss comes to all of us. The trick is in learning how to bend and not break, which is probably as great a lesson in life as learning to attach.

Torey's goal in forming relationships with her children, as stated various times through her books, is to help more than she hurts. That's all any of us can aim for, as the perfect person or perfect relationship does not exist. We remain committed to the idea that we all do need to know in a very real way that we matter to someone, someplace, even if we cannot be together. And real love, for whatever time it lasts, is never wasted.

References

Anderson, J. A., Kyutash, K., & Duchnowski, A. J. (2001). A comparison of the academic progress of students with EBD and students with LD. *Journal of Emotional and Behavioral Disorders, 9*, 106–115.

APA Working Group on Psychoactive Medications for Children and Adolescents. (2006). *Report of the Working Group on Psychoactive Medications for Children and Adolescents: Psychopharmacological, psychosocial, and combined interventions for childhood disorders: Evidence base, contextual factors, and future directions.* Washington, DC: American Psychological Association.

Benson, H. (2000). *The relaxation response.* New York, NY: HarperTorch.

Bradley, R., Henderson, K., & Monfore, D. A. (2004). A national perspective on children with emotional disorders. *Behavioral Disorders, 29*, 211–223.

Breggin, P. (2000). *Reclaiming our children: A healing plan for a nation in crisis.* Cambridge, MA: Perseus Books.

Breggin, P. (2008). *Medication madness.* New York, NY: St. Martin's Press.

Brendtro, L. K. (2008). Wings: The legacy. *Reclaiming Children and Youth, 17*(2), 11–18.

Brendtro, L. K., & Brokenleg, M. (2007). Beyond the curriculum of control. In N. J. Long, W. C. Morse, F. A. Fecser, & R. G. Newman (Eds.), *Conflict in the classroom* (6th ed., pp. 88–101). Austin, TX: Pro-Ed.

Brendtro, L. K., Brokenleg, M., & Van Bockern, S. (2002). *Reclaiming youth at risk: Our hope for the future.* Thousand Oaks, CA: Solution Tree.

Brendtro, L. K., Mitchell, M. L., & McCall, H. J. (2009). *Deep brain learning: Pathways to potential with challenging youth.* Albion, MI: Starr Commonwealth.

Bruner, J. S. (1985). Narrative and paradigmatic modes of thought. In E. Eisner (Ed.), *Learning and teaching the ways of knowing* (84th yearbook of the National Society for the Study of Education, pp. 97–115). Chicago, IL: University of Chicago Press.

Bruner, J. S. (2002). *Making stories: Law, literature, and life.* Cambridge, MA: Harvard University.

Cambone, J. (1994). *Teaching troubled children: A case study in effective classroom practice.* New York, NY: Teachers College Press.

Cook, B. G. (2012). Evidence-based practice and practice based evidence: A union of insufficiencies. *FOCUS on Research, 24*(4), 1–2.

Corey, G. (2000). *Theory and practice of counseling and psychotherapy* (6th ed.). Pacific Grove, CA: Brooks/Cole.

Cozolino, L. (2006). *The neuroscience of human relationships: Attachment and the developing social brain.* New York, NY: W. W. Norton.

Danforth, S., & Smith, T. J. (2005). *Engaging troubling students: A constructivist approach.* Thousand Oaks, CA: Corwin.

Foltz, R. (2008). Medicating relational trauma in youth. *Reclaiming Children and Youth, 17*(3), 3–8.

Foltz, R. (2012). Twenty years of medicating youth: Are we better off? *Reclaiming Children and Youth, 20*(4), 31–36.

Gardner, H. (2006). *Multiple intelligences: New horizons in theory and practice.* New York, NY: Basic Books.

Garfat, T. (2010). The truth in their experience: The evidence from youth and families. *Reclaiming Children and Youth, 19*(2), 55–57.

Gilbert, A.G. (1977). *Teaching the three Rs through movement experiences.* Minneapolis, MN: Burgess Publishing Company.

Goldstein, A. P., & McGinnis, E. (1997). *Skillstreaming the adolescent: A structured learning approach to teaching prosocial skills* (2nd ed.). Champaign, IL: Research Press.

Hayden, T. L. (1980). *One child.* New York, NY: Avon Press.

Hayden, T. L. (1982). *Somebody else's kids.* New York, NY: Avon Press.

Hayden, T. L. (1983). *Murphy's boy.* New York, NY: Avon Press.

Hayden, T. L. (1986). *Just another kid.* New York, NY: Avon Press.

Hayden, T. L. (1992). *Ghost girl.* New York, NY: Avon Press.

Hayden, T. L. (1995). *The tiger's child.* New York, NY: Avon Press.

Hayden, T. L. (2001, September). Attachment and loss [Online forum comment]. Retrieved from http://www.torey-hayden.com/Message board/Our archives/Torey's books

Hayden, T. L. (2002). *Beautiful child.* New York, NY: Avon Press.

Hayden, T. L. (2005). *Twilight children.* New York, NY: Avon Press.

Hobbs, N. (1994). *The troubled and troubling child.* Cleveland, OH: American Re-Education Association.

Hubble, M., Duncan, & Miller, S. (1999). *The heart and soul of change.* Washington, DC: American Psychological Association.

International Narcotics Control Board. (2007). Report of the International Narcotics Control Board for 2007. Retrieved from http://www.medscape.com/viewarticle/541762

Kauffman, J. M., & Hallahan, D. P. (2005). *The illusion of full inclusion: A comprehensive critique of a current special education bandwagon* (2nd ed.). Austin, TX: Pro-Ed.

Kauffman, J. M., & Landrum, T. (2009). *Characteristics of emotional and behavioral disorders of children and youth* (7th ed.). Upper Saddle River, NJ: Merrill/Prentice Hall.

Kirsch, I. (2010). *The emperor's new drugs: Exploding the antidepressant myth.* New York, NY: Basic Books.

Knitzer, J., Steinberg, Z., & Fleish, F. (1990). *At the schoolhouse door. An examination of the programs and policies for children with behavioral and emotional problems.* New York, NY: Bank Street College of Education.

Kohlberg, L. (1981). *The philosophy of moral development: Moral stages and the idea of justice* (Vol. 1). New York, NY: Harper & Row, Publishers.

Lane, K. L., Barton-Arwood, S. M., Nelson, J. R., & Wehby, J. H. (2008). Academic performance of children with emotional and behavioral disorders served in a self-contained setting. *Journal of Behavioral Education, 17,* 43–62.

Long, N. J. (2008). Breaking the trust barrier with troubled students. *Reclaiming Children and Youth, 17*(1), 57–58.

Maag, J. W. (2006). Social skills training for students with emotional and behavioral disorders: A review of reviews. *Behavioral Disorders, 32,* 4–17.

Maggin, D. M., Wehby, J. H., Moore Partin, T. C., Robertson, R., & Oliver, R. M. (2011). A comparison of the instructional context for students with behavioral issues enrolled in self-contained and general education classrooms. *Behavioral Disorders, 36,* 84–99.

Marlowe, M. (1999). Reaching reluctant students: Insights from Torey Hayden. *Reclaiming Children and Youth, 7*(4), 242–245, 254.

Marlowe, M. (2006, April). *The phenomenology of reading Torey Hayden's stories in teacher education.* Paper presented at the Annual Conference on College Teaching and Learning, Jacksonville, FL.

Marlowe, M., & Disney, G. (2007). A study of the long-term influence of Torey Hayden's teacher lore on teachers' attitudes and practices toward children with disabilities. In J. Butcher & L. McDonald (Eds.), *Making a difference: Challenges for teachers, teaching, and teacher education* (pp. 205–219). Rotterdam, the Netherlands: Sense Publishers.

Marlowe, M. & Maycock, G. (2000). Phenomenology of bibliotherapy in modifying teacher punitiveness. *The Journal of Genetic Psychology, 161,* 325–336.

Marlowe, M. & Maycock, G. (2001). Using literary texts in teacher education to promote positive attitudes toward children with disabilities. *Teacher Education and Special Education, 24,* 75–83.

Marlowe, M., Maycock, G., Palmer, L., & Morrison, W. (1997). Using literary texts in teacher education to promote positive attitudes toward children with emotional and behavioral disorders. *Behavioral Disorders, 22,* 152–159.

Morris, G. S. D., & Stiehl, J. (1999). *Changing kids' games.* Champaign, IL: Research Press.

Morse, W. C. (2008). *Connecting with kids in conflict: A life space legacy.* Sioux Falls, SD: Reclaiming Children and Youth and Starr Commonwealth.

Mott, B. W., McQuiggan, S. W., Lee, S., Lee, S. Y., & Lester, J. (2006). Narrative centered environments for guided discovery learning. In *Proceedings of the Textual Case-Based Reasoning Workshop at the 5th International Joint Conference on Autonomous Agents and Multi-agent Systems* (pp. 67–82). Hakodate, Japan: Association for Computer Machinery.

Mulrine, C. F., Prater, M. A., & Jenkins, A. (2008). The active classroom: Supporting students with attention deficit hyperactivity disorder through exercise. *TEACHING Exceptional Children, 40,* 16–23.

Nelson, J. R., Benner, G. J., Lane, K., & Smith, B. W. (2004). Academic achievement of K–12 students with emotional and behavioral disorders. *Exceptional Children, 71,* 59–63.

Nichols, P. (2007). The curriculum of control: Twelve reasons for it, some arguments against it. In N. J. Long, W. C. Morse, F. A. Fecser, & R. G. Newman (Eds.), *Conflict in the classroom* (6th ed., pp. 88–101). Austin, TX: Pro-Ed.

Noddings, N. (1991). Stories in dialogue. In C. Witherall & N. Noddings (Eds.), *Stories lives tell: Narrative and dialogue in education* (pp. 157–170). New York, NY: Teachers College Press.

Noddings, N. (2003). *Caring: A feminine approach to ethics and moral education* (2nd ed.). Berkely: University of California Press.

Perry, B., & Szalavitz, M. (2006). *The boy who was raised as a dog: What traumatized children can teach us about love, loss, and healing.* New York, NY: Basic Books.

Pianata, R. C. (1999). *Enhancing relationships between children and teachers.* Washington, DC: American Psychological Association.

Poulton, A. (2005). Growth on stimulant medication: Clarifying the confusion: A review. *Archives of Disease in Childhood, 90*, 801–806.

Regan, K. S. (2003). Using dialogue journals in the classroom: Forming relationships with students with emotional disturbances. *TEACHING Exceptional Children, 36*, 36–41.

Reid, R., Gonzalez, J. E., Nordness, P. D., Trout, A., & Epstein, M. H. (2004). A meta-analysis of the academic status of students with emotional/behavioral disturbance. *Journal of Special Education, 38*, 130–143.

Resnick, M., Bearman, P., Blum, R., Bauman, K., Harris, K., Jones, R., . . . Udry, J. (1997). Protecting adolescents from harm: Findings from the national longitudinal study on adolescent health. *Journal of the American Medical Association, 278*, 823–832.

Ryan, J., Reid, R., Gallagher, K., & Ellis, C. (2008). Prevalence rate of psychotropic medications for students placed in residential facilities. *Behavioral Disorders, 33*, 99–107.

Sapon-Shevin, M. (2007). *Widening the circle: The power of inclusive classrooms.* Boston, MA: Beacon Press.

Seita, J., Mitchell, M., & Tobin, C. (1996). *In whose best interest?* Elizabethtown, PA: Continental Press.

Siperstein, G. N., Wiley, A. L., & Forness, S. R. (2011). School context and the academic and behavioral progress of students with emotional disturbance. *Behavioral Disorders, 36*, 172–184.

Special Education Elementary Longitudinal Study (SEELS). (2003). *Facts from OSEP's national longitudinal studies: Use of psychotropic medication by children and youth with disabilities.* Menlo Park, CA: SRI International.

Steele, W. (2009). Drawing: An evidence based intervention for trauma victims. *Reclaiming Children and Youth, 18*(1), 20–23.

Szalavitz, M., & Perry, B. (2010). *Born for love: Why empathy is essential—and endangered.* New York, NY: HarperCollins.

United States Department of Education. (2006). *Twenty-sixth annual report to Congress on the implementation of the*

Individuals with Disabilities Education Act, 2004. Washington, DC: Author.

Valore, C. L. (2007). Spitting from windmills: The therapeutic value of effective instruction. In N.J. Long, W. C. Morse, F. A. Fecser, & R. G. Newman (Eds.). *Conflict in the classroom* (6th ed., pp. 212–221). Austin, TX: Pro-Ed.

VanderVen, K. (2009). Why focusing on control backfires: A systems perspective. *Reclaiming Children and Youth, 17*(4), 8–12.

Vigilone, N. (2009). Applying art and action. *Reclaiming Children and Youth, 18*(1), 16–19.

Vitto, J. M. (2003). *Relationship-driven classroom management.* Thousand Oaks, CA: Corwin.

Werner, E., & Smith, R. (1992). *Overcoming the odds.* Ithaca, NY: Cornell University Press.

Wiseman, R. (2003). *The luck factor: The scientific study of the lucky mind.* London: Century.

Zigmond, N., & Kloo, A. (2011). General and special education are (and should be) different. In J. M. Kauffman & D. P. Hallahan (Eds.), *Handbook of special education* (pp. 160–172). New York, NY: Routledge.

Zins, J., Elias, M., Weissberg, R., Greenberg, M., Haynes, N., & Frey, K. (1998). Enhancing learning through social and emotional education. *CASEL Collections, 2,* 1–3.

Index

CORWIN

A SAGE Company

The Corwin logo—a raven striding across an open book—represents the union of courage and learning. Corwin is committed to improving education for all learners by publishing books and other professional development resources for those serving the field of PreK–12 education. By providing practical, hands-on materials, Corwin continues to carry out the promise of its motto: **"Helping Educators Do Their Work Better."**